ENRICHING THE RUNIC TRADITION

"A highly concentrated, well-integrated and rational system of rune magic. Cooper introduces thought-provoking personal interpretations of the runes that yield many fresh insights into their hidden meanings and magical uses. Of particular interest is his system for carving and painting the runes to release their occult potency."

— Donald Tyson
author of *Ritual Magic, The New Magus,*
and *How to Make and Use a Magic Mirror*

"If you are curious about the old Germanic runes and the spiritual insight attributed to their mere contemplation, then this is the book for you. Jason Cooper's impressive research and guidelines save questing students months, if not years, in acquiring the craft and knowledge for themselves."

— G. M. Glaskin
author of *The Christos Experience* Trilogy

"Esoteric Rune Magic, with its emphasis on personal runic growth via myth-making and practical exercises, is an extremely valuable addition to the library of any rune vitki."

— Lisa Peschel
author of *A Practical Guide to the Runes*

ABOUT THE AUTHOR

D. Jason Cooper was born December 9, 1957, in Fort Erie, a small Canadian town, but grew up just across the border in Buffalo, New York. In 1977 he moved to Perth, Australia, and lives there with his wife Sue, daughter Shadra, and son Darius. This is his third book and his second on the runes.

He has been interested in the philosophical, occult, and metaphysical since late grade school. He is a voracious student of occultism, Paganism, and new age philosophy and is the head of a small esoteric group, the Companions of the Phoenix.

TO WRITE TO THE AUTHOR

If you wish to contact the author or would like more information about this book, please write to the author in care of Llewellyn Worldwide, and we will forward your request. Both the author and publisher appreciate hearing from you and learning of your enjoyment of this book and how it has helped you. Llewellyn Worldwide cannot guarantee that every letter written to the author can be answered, but all will be forwarded. Please write to:

D. Jason Cooper
c/o Llewellyn Worldwide
P.O. Box 64383-K174, St. Paul, MN 55164-0383, U.S.A.

Please enclosed a self-addressed, stamped envelope or $1.00 to cover costs.
If outside the U.S.A., enclose international postal reply coupon.

FREE CATALOG FROM LLEWELLYN

For more than 90 years Llewellyn has brought its readers knowledge in the fields of metaphysics and human potential. Learn about the newest books in spiritual guidance, natural healing, astrology, occult philosophy, and more. Enjoy book reviews, new age articles, a calendar of events, plus current advertised products and services. To get your free copy of *Llewellyn's New Worlds of Mind and Spirit*, send your name and address to:

Llewellyn's New Worlds of Mind and Spirit
P.O. Box 64383-K174, St. Paul, MN 55164-0383, U.S.A.

WORLD MAGIC SERIES

ESOTERIC RUNE MAGIC

The Elder Futhark in Magic,
Astral Projection and
Spiritual Development

D. JASON COOPER

1994
Llewellyn Publications
St. Paul, MN 55164-0383, U.S.A.

FIRST EDITION
Second Printing, 1994

Cover art: Scott Fray
Interior art: Linda Norton
Book design and layout: Jessica Thoreson

Library of Congress Cataloging-in-Publication Data
Cooper, D. Jason.
    Esoteric rune magic: the elder futhark in magic, astral
    projection and spiritual development / D. Jason Cooper.
       p.   cm. — (Llewellyn's world magic series)
    Includes bibliographical references and index.
    ISBN 1-56718-174-0
    1. Runes—Miscellanea. 2. Magic, Germanic. 3. Magic.
    I. Title. II. Series.
    BF1623.R89C67   1994
    133.3'3—dc20   94-10749
                                        CIP

Printed in the United States of America

Llewellyn Publications
A Division of Llewellyn Worldwide, Ltd.
P.O. Box 64383, St. Paul, MN 55164-0383

LLEWELLYN'S WORLD MAGIC SERIES

At the core of every religion, at the foundation of every culture, there is MAGIC.

Magic sees the world as alive, as the home which humanity shares with beings and powers both visible and invisible with whom and which we can interface to either our advantage or disadvantage—depending upon our awareness and intention.

Religious worship and communion is one kind of magic, and just as there are many religions in the world, so are there many magical systems.

Religion and magic are ways of seeing and relating to the creative powers, the living energies, the all-pervading spirit, the underlying intelligence that is the universe within which we and all else exist.

Neither religion nor magic conflicts with science. All share the same goals and the same limitations: always seeking truth, and forever haunted by human limitations in perceiving that truth. Magic is "technology" based upon experience and extrasensory insight, providing its practitioners with methods of greater influence and control over the world of the invisible before it impinges on the world of the visible.

The study of world magic not only enhances your understanding of the world in which you live, and hence your ability to live better, but brings you into touch with the inner essence of your long evolutionary heritage and most particularly—as in the case of the magical system identified most closely with your genetic inheritance—with the archetypal images and forces most alive in your whole consciousness.

To Dianne
for magic

TABLE OF CONTENTS

INTRODUCTION

There are three major magical alphabets used by Western occultists: the Hebrew alphabet, the Enochian alphabet, and the runes, or Futhark. Our subject is the last of these alphabets.

Last, but not least. The Futhark is as potent and significant a magical alphabet as any other. But it does differ from the other two in several significant respects, particularly in relation to the development of practical magic.

The magic of the Enochian and Hebrew alphabets depends on abstruse, recondite patterns of correspondences. These patterns relate to a vast cosmological apparatus which has to be understood before magical results can really be expected.

This means that the student or spellcaster must spend long periods of time and make a significant effort to learn the nature of these alphabets before they can be used for magic. The runes of the Futhark are quite the opposite—they can be used immediately in practical magic.

This is not to say the Futhark is simplistic. It has as complex, as deep, and as valid a mythographic structure as the other two alphabets. But the path of learning about that structure, the means of entering it, is entirely different. It is this different structure that makes the Futhark more accessible.

There are three major (and several minor) variations of the Futhark. These are the Germanic or Elder, the Scandinavian or Norse, and the Anglo-Saxon.

In this book we are working with the Elder or Germanic Futhark. It is the oldest of the three, and the most sophisticated magically. The runes of the Elder Futhark are divided into three "aettir," or families, named after the gods Freyja, Heimdall, and Tir. The importance of this division has been overlooked by modern writers, but it reflects the depth of philosophical understanding which lies behind the runes.

We're not certain when the runes originated. The name "Futhark" is used because the first six letters of the Germanic runes are f, u, th, a, r, and k. The variant in which we are interested was used most widely between the fifth and eighth centuries. Its first use has been set variously at the third or first century AD or even the first century BC—the time when Rome was building its empire.

We do know that the runes were used over a wide area. From Normandy to southern Lithuania, from the German-Danish border to the north of Italy, the Germanic Futhark was used for magic, poetry, and even for legal documents.

We know of a sword inscribed with the rune tyr, and others with the runic inscriptions "increase to pain" and "woe to enemies." But in addition to this battle magic, the runes were used for healing, for success, and for bringing love. They were a practical form of magic for all aspects of ordinary human life.

They were also used for divination and the more recondite magics of priests. They opened the gateways to magic for the Germanic peoples—shamanic magic which itself harkened back centuries.

H. R. Ellis-Davison has shown that many of the Germanic pagan myths and gods go back to the Bronze Age. The one-handed god, for example, is seen in rock carvings of that age. The Norse view of the world tree (Yggdrasil) holding up a sky made of a giant's skull may predate the modern human race.

In Neanderthal camps some elements of religious beliefs or magic have been found. These include a deer carcass sprinkled with red dust with stone tools inside it, and a ring of stones in the center of which is a wooden stake. On the top of that stake sits a human (Neanderthal) skull.

The runes of the Futhark are not that old, however. They probably originated with a magical genius who used them to coordinate a number of disparate ideas of Germanic paganism into a whole, much as S. L. MacGregor-Mathers took a variety of elements from Western occultism and synthesized them into the material of the Golden Dawn.

We don't know the name of this genius, but he seems to have been a single individual. He probably was a local tribal ruler who used the shamanistic cult as one of the pillars to his rule, and the runes as a pillar of the cult.

Where he settled we cannot be sure, but Denmark or southern Sweden is the most likely location. His autocracy led to his overthrow by a Dane named Oller. But he regained his throne (possibly after a time of wandering) and on his death was deified. In deification he may have been merged with a local deity named Od, whose name may have been the same or nearly the same as that of the man.

It is even possible that the introduction of the runes was the method of his gaining the backing of a cult of shamans, and hence regaining the throne.

In myth, the god Odin gained the runes. He did not invent them, but won them through ordeal. The nature of the ordeal is in line with patterns of initiation among primitive tribes. In the myth, Odin hung from a windswept tree for nine days and nights. He hung by his thumbs, wounded in the side by a spear. Then he saw the worlds below him, which we can take to mean he had a vision, and shrieking, took up the runes.

The word "rune" comes from proto-Germanic and means "to roar." So the name probably derives from the original act at the time of the vision. Once Odin screamed he was given a drink—possibly a hallucinogen—to enhance the vision.

When he arose, or at some time shortly thereafter, he promulgated his new vision of paganism. The cult of Odin was different from anything that had gone before it. The runes formed a unifying set of magical devices.

Note that the runes, in whatever Futhark we wish to examine, are unique in the world of letters. They are the only letter system without curved lines. Every line is straight.

It has been suggested that this is because the runes were frequently carved into wood. But we have examples of runes written on paper and these have no curves. Moreover, Germanic carving and metalwork shows no avoidance of curves in any other case.

It is clear both historically and magically that the individual strokes of the runes were devices for enhancing their magic. They were mnemonic devices allowing the followers of the cult of Odin to unify and deepen Germanic paganism.

It is important to realize when the *lay* (poem) has Odin say he "looked down" and "took up" the runes, it is being quite literal. The runes are a combination of two things. The first of these is the traditional magical stone carvings of the Germanic pagans. These carvings, now called the Hallristing carvings, were used in Germanic paganism as long ago as the Bronze Age, or possibly longer. These traditional carvings were combined with one or more of the several alphabets descended from the Phoenician alphabet—the Roman, Greek, and Etruscan alphabets are the most likely candidates.

That such a combination occurred is suggested by several things. Chief among is them that some runes closely resemble known letters and are associated with similar sounds. So boerc looks like a Roman B but is made of angular lines and sounds like a B.

Other runes closely resemble Hallristing carvings. There are 18 runes which seem to be based on these carvings or other magical images—that is, not based on the Greek or Roman alphabets. In the original poem in which the runes are discovered, 18 spells are described. In several cases, the description of the spells closely matches the use of the runes in question.

The Futhark devised became the basis of the new cult of Odin, originally run by him and, on his death, dedicated to him as the god Odin. The god Odin displaced Tiwaz or Tir at the head of the pantheon. Tiwaz was the ancient Aryan god Dayus, familiar to many branches of the tribe. To the Greeks, for example, he was Zeus; to the Romans, Deus Pitar or Jupiter.

ᚠᚢᚦᚨᚱᚲᚷᚹᚺᚾᛁᛃᛇᛈᛉᛊᛏᛒᛖᛗᛚᛜᛞᚠᚢᚦᚨᚱᚲᚷᚹᚺᚾᛁᛃᛇᛈᛉᛊᛏᛒ

Odin's cult continued until the eleventh or even twelfth century. At that time an inquisition was instituted against Germanic paganism. It is possible that the cult lasted another century or two underground—if Jews can survive underground for 500 years in Portugal, why should paganism be any less resilient?

Aside from that, material survived. There were some myths preserved in the *Elder Edda*, the *Prose Edda*, the *Gesta Danorum*, and Tacitus' *Germania*. From the nineteenth century on there has been an increasing interest in the sites of ancient paganism. Archaeologists have continued to improve research techniques, gaining a greater ability to discover and decipher the physical remnants of that pagan era.

This increasing knowledge has been of tremendous help to occultists interested in the runes of the Futhark or Germanic paganism in general. But the technologies of magic have not remained unchanged. These advances have been applied to the runes, developing their abilities.

For example, the traditional runes had one color—red. This pigment was used for all runes, and seems to have been descended from the symbolic use of red soil during the Palae-olithic (Old Stone) Age. Now we use color as an enhancement of the runes. Basically the same scheme of attribution appeared independently on at least two occasions.

The old cipher of runes, the "twig" runes, has formed the basis of an extensive and highly useful exploration of the runes through numerology.

These studies have helped uncover the original genius of the runes. They are not just images, they are also focal points of power. Each stroke has its own symbolic value and can be a part of the ritual of creating the rune.

The Futhark used today is similar to that used as many as 2,100 years ago. But the runes are different. They have advanced, progressed, and developed in line with human evolution so this magic which predates humanity is also ready for the twenty-first century.

The uses of the runes are many. The runes of the Futhark can be used for meditation or astral projection, and if summoned properly as a method of harnessing magical power. It is even possible to combine runes into very specific devices of power.

For each of these uses no special tools except your own abilities will be necessary. If you prefer, however, a runeplace can be made. This book will take you through all the steps you need to gain runic wisdom. We'll begin by examining each of the runes of the Elder Futhark.

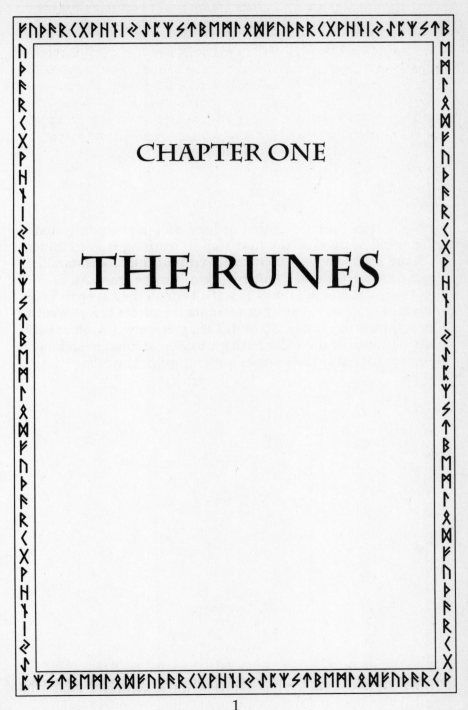

CHAPTER ONE

THE RUNES

No matter how integrated or how deep and complicated a magical system is, the first step in learning it is to understand the individual elements. Without this understanding, magic degenerates into wonder-working for the ignorant.

This is true of the runes as well. Though they are part of an integrated system, we must understand the pieces before we can hope to know the whole. So in this chapter we will look at each of the 24 runes of the Elder Futhark to gain an understanding of their magical nature as a preparation for magical work.

Name: Feoh
Phonetic Value: F
Aett: Freyja
Number: 1 in aett 1
Color: Brown
Source: Hallristing carving—ᛉ

Image: Feoh represents a cow or bull, possibly one under yoke, either before plowing or before sacrifice on a feast day.

Esoteric Meaning: Feoh refers to domesticated cattle, though a general reference to livestock should be accepted. As such it is a sign of wealth and prosperity not only of the individual but also of society.

Remember that the wealthy members of pagan societies provided the animals for the meat of holiday feasts. In this way the nutritional needs of the poor were at least partially fulfilled in a way that created no social stigma.

The animals were also feted rather more than the trussed creatures killed in modern slaughterhouses. They were often garlanded. The method of execution was as follows: a log suspended by chains was drawn back; when released, it swung into the animal's head and stunned the creature. This chased out any demons that might have inhabited the animal and ensured that its death was as painless as possible.

Feoh is a sign of hope and plenty, success and happiness; it also indicates the responsibilities of those at the top, and a social binding for all levels.

Magical Uses: This rune provides success, advancement in career, and a turnabout in luck for those in difficulty. The good luck it provides is not permanent, but a single event or a short period of good fortune. After that the charm must be renewed, not only magically but through an act of binding or connection in the social sense.

This act can be a gift to charity, help to another, or some other action to link oneself to a social order. The rune is good for areas of money, friendliness, and gaining merit.

ᛗᛗᛚᚱᛘᚠᚾᛚᚠᚱᚲᚷᛈᚺᛏᛁᛇᛋᚲᚲᛇᛋᛏᛒᛗᛗᛚᚱᛘᚠᚾᛚᚠᚱᚲᚷᛈᚺᛏᛁᛇᛋ

This combined with beneficence is reminiscent of the eighth rune mentioned by Odin in the poem in which he describes his winning of the runes. There it is described as a rune which uproots hate in people's minds.

Associated God: Freyja, the Vanir goddess.

Freyja is known for her kindness. She is invoked for marriage, love, and seduction, but she is also a goddess of plenty. In her functions she combines many aspects of the rune.

Freyja appears as a woman in her early to middle twenties. She is a goddess of flashing eyes and full lips. She wears a catskin hood that covers her hair, white calfskin gloves, and brown calfskin boots. Her dress is a tunic of white linen embroidered with gold; this does not cover her legs. Her cloak is made of hawk's feathers and reaches to the ground.

Individual Strokes: When carving, first do the upper diagonal from right to left, going down. Then the lower diagonal is carved up and to the right. Finally, the vertical is carved from bottom to top.

When coloring, start with the vertical stroke; color this from bottom to top. The lower diagonal is colored down and to the left, then the upper diagonal is colored from left to right.

Note that the diagonals are always carved or colored in opposite directions. This maintains the symbolism of the exchange inherent in the rune. The vertical is carved and colored from bottom to top, indicating a rise in fortune. The diagonals are part of the lesson "a gift demands a gift," the structure of society. The vertical is the increase in personal benefit.

As each stroke is carved, recite the following:

> *Good things given*
> *good things received,*
> *pleasure in life is maintained.*

ᚠᚢᚦᚨᚱᚲᚷᚹᚺᚾᛁᛃᛇᛈᛉᛊᛏᛒᛖᛗᛚᛜᛞᚠᚢᚦᚨᚱᚲᚷᚹᚺᛁᛃᛇᛊᛏᛒ

Name: Ur
Phonetic Value: U
Aett: Freyja
Number: 2 in aett 1
Color: Green, particularly dark green
Source: Hallristing carving—

Image: Ur represents a wild ox, as opposed to the domesticated beast of feoh. It is a reminder of the primeval cow, Adumla, who licked the brine of the world before time. Doing so, it freed Odin's grandfather and suckled him.

The image here is of an ox with its horns down before charging, but it is also the great flow of creativity from the upper left-hand point.

Esoteric Meaning: A wild ox, denoting the untamed powers of creativity and immediacy. This primal power does not come without danger.

Magical Uses: Ur is useful for releasing creativity and creating sudden change. It can be used to release or tame power. In all cases there is a certain danger to the action, since it will be the runecaster's personal skill and power which will control that which is unleashed.

In conjunction with other runes, ur is useful in the evocation of various natural powers. It helps in areas of risk and beginning an adventure, even that of starting a business or any other area in which you are putting something at risk.

In the eighteen runes of which Odin speaks, the sixteenth is one that wins the heart of a woman. This sense of taming a woman was endemic in the attitudes of Aesir gods and their followers.

Associated God: Adumla, the primeval cow.

Adumla appears in various forms in many of the mythologies of the descendants of the Aryan tribes. The sacred cow of India is well known. But in Iranian mythology, according to the prophet Zoroaster, the cow has a soul which addresses the Wise Lord, Ahura Mazda. In the religion of Mithras, that deity slays

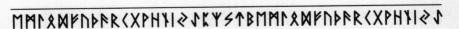

the sacred cow to unleash its creative power. Adumla is not only power, but the ability to nurture.

Individual Strokes: To carve the rune, start at the upper left-hand corner. Carve the diagonal stroke down and to the right. Then carve the right-hand vertical stroke down. Then carve the left-hand vertical stroke from top to bottom.

To color the rune, start at the bottom of the left-hand stroke and color upward. Then color the right-hand vertical from top to bottom, and connect the two by coloring the diagonal stroke downward from left to right.

In the carving everything flows from the original point, the dominant point in the structure. All things initially form from it. In the coloring the dominant point is approached with the first stroke; the independent, parallel force of the other vertical is brought "under control" by the diagonal.

The words here are:

> *Danger and force*
> *I do face,*
> *and win.*

ᚠᚢᚦᚨᚱᚲᚷᚹᚺᚾᛁᛖᛃᛊᛏᚳᛃᛋᛒᛗᛗᛚᛉᛞᚠᚢᚦᚨᚱᚲᚷᚹᚺᚾᛁᛖᛃᛋᛏᛒ

Name: Thorn
Phonetic Value: The voiceless th of theory
Aett: Freyja
Number: 3 in aett 1
Color: White (can be colored light gray if necessary)
Source: Hallristing carving— ↑
Image: Thorn is the name and symbol of an ice demon. The rune itself is its magical sigil.

Esoteric Meaning: Thorn lived in the most remote parts of the forests, where it could devour unwary travellers who crossed its path. Such fears are common among peoples who live scattered in the wilderness. Some Native American tribes feared a demon called the Wendigo, a creature surprisingly similar to thorn.

For Germanic tribes winter was a time of privation; the rune symbolized that. But it was also the sign of the frost and ice giants, creatures who fought against the gods and human beings alike.

Magical Uses: Thorn is useful for attack and sometimes for tests. It makes people careless at the wrong moment; it makes people sicken; it drives people insane. It is particularly suitable for increasing the fear of people already afraid.

Of Odin's list of eighteen runes, the sixth turns an enemy's spells against them. In the poem the spell is stated to be the root of a sapling with runes cut into it.

Associated God: Hel and the dragon Nidhogg.

Hel was the daughter of Loki and the ruler of Niflheim, the land of the dead. She ruled over those who died of disease, of old age, or who lived evil lives. Hers was a land of darkness filled with animated corpses, serpents, and a poisonous mist that limited vision. In Niflheim, even gold rots.

Hel appears as a woman who is very beautiful and extremely pale from head to waist. From the waist down she is a green-black and pink rotting corpse. Maggots crawl across this part of her, pus breaks out here and there, and sores open that sometimes go down to the bone. Hel is always naked.

Nidhogg was the dragon who ate at the root of the world tree, Yggdrasil. This chewing would one day bring the tree down, signaling the beginning of Ragnarok.

Nidhogg appears as a vast dragon who can only be partially seen. He has shiny, metallic scales, but in the darkness of Niflheim the color of these is hard to detect—if indeed they have any definite color.

From his maw drip poison, saliva, froth, and pieces of the Yggdrasil at which Nidhogg constantly chews.

Individual Strokes: To carve this rune, start with the upper diagonal and carve down and to the right. Then make the vertical stroke from top to bottom. Finally, the lower diagonal is carved down from right to left.

To color the rune, start by making the vertical stroke straight down. Then the upper diagonal is colored down and to the right, and the lower diagonal down and to the left.

In this there is no source or meeting of the rune. In carving and coloring, all three strokes travel down, but there is no continuity of the strokes.

During carving and coloring these are the lines to use:

Alone am I
when I face danger
but never do I falter.

ᚠᚢᚦᚨᚱᚲᚷᚹᚺᚾᛁᛃᛇᛈᛉᛋᛏᛒᛖᛗᛚᛜᛞᚠᚢᚦᚨᚱᚲᚷᚺᚾᛁᛃᛇᛋᛏᛒ

Name: Os

Phonetic Value: Depending on accent, somewhere between a short A and a short O.

Aett: Freyja

Number: 4 in aett 1

Color: Purple

Source: Hallristing carving—↑

Image: Pictograph of a pine tree.

Esoteric Meaning: Pine trees, being hermaphroditic, are symbolic of immortality and the divine impulse of human beings. They were symbols of the gods.

The word "os" means god, goddess, or deity and ultimately comes from the Indo-European word *dayus*, which indicates both daylight and deity.

In Odin's list of eighteen runes, the fourteenth tells the names of the gods and the elves one by one.

Magical Uses: This is a rune of luck, good fortune, and the invocation of divine power or help. Compare this to the rune thorn, which calls upon the chaotic or evil powers of the universe.

Os is also good for writing poetry or prose or for success in public speaking.

Associated God: All gods, but particularly Odin.

Germanic gods, unlike many of their Greco-Roman or Egyptian counterparts, are not limited to a single godform. Odin, for example, has three. The one which applies to this rune is Odin as All-Father, god of the sky and ruler of the other deities.

He wears a mailcoat of black leather and brass, a helmet with two horns, and a metal eyepatch on his right eye. He carries a spear, Gungnir, which is slightly taller than he is. The spear tip has a flange on either side, and etched into the head and flanges is a raven in flight. He wears animal-skin trousers and boots.

His hair is steel gray and a raven sits on either shoulder. By either foot is a wolf.

This is Odin of hosts, giver of victory. But he can be a treacherous god, and one should be careful not to rob him of his share of the spoils.

He is also the all-seeing god, wise and able. He can be called upon to give knowledge of the divine realm.

Individual Strokes: First carve the vertical stroke downward. Then carve the lower diagonal from left to right and downward, then the upper diagonal from right to left and upward.

Color the rune by starting the vertical stroke upward, then the lower diagonal from left to right and downward. Finally, the upper diagonal is colored from right to left and upward.

The carving shows power or wisdom coming from above with an exchange in the diagonals. The coloring shows the invocation from below moving upward, and exchange, again, in the diagonals. Compare this to feoh: in both cases there is a transfer across levels within a structure of exchange.

The words to recite for this are as follows:

Divine power is called.
Divine grace is asked.
Call forth the gods.

ᚠᚢᚦᚨᚱᚲᚷᚹᚺᚾᛁᛃᛇᛈᛉᛊᛏᛒᛖᛗᛚᛜᚠᚢᚦᚨᚱᚲᚷᚹᚺᚾᛁᛃᛇᛈᛉᛊᛏᛒ

Name: Rad

Phonetic Value: R

Aett: Freyja

Number: 5 in aett 1

Color: Black

Source: The Roman letter R

Image: A man on horseback at night, riding in a night sky into an invisible doorway to another world.

Esoteric Meaning: Rad signifies the journey into the underworld. Throughout the world shamans do not walk into the underworld, nor enter it under their own power. They ride an animal or, in some cases, a cart. For Odin the trip was made on Sleipnir, the eight-legged horse some said was four men carrying a coffin. Freyja used the form of a hawk. Thor drove a cart pulled by two goats.

Magical Uses: This rune symbolizes the journey to a place of power, the realms of the dead. Thus it can be used to gain knowledge from the dead through necromancy, seance, and divination.

It is also useful for promoting change, unblocking stymied situations, and hallowing things. It can be used to bless, in both a positive and negative sense.

A negative blessing is simply an injunction against dark forces, much like the Orthodox "God save you from all demons." But it can also be used to invoke positive forces. In both cases there is a link to the dead who have positive or negative wisdom for and intentions toward us.

It is good for understanding great changes, anything to do with ancestors (apart from inheritance), traveling in safety, and immigration.

Associated God: Thor, the Thunderer.

Thor was a thunder god, which is certainly in keeping with a rune of great change. But he was also the god of hallowing, community, and travel. Odin may have been a god of (male) nobility, but Thor was the god of the yeoman farmer, the merchant, and the adventurer. These are people who depend upon the principles of change, and upon hallowing to give them luck during the change.

He should be seen as a big man, seven or eight feet tall. He has unkempt bright red hair and beard. He is usually bareheaded, though he sometimes wears an unadorned iron helmet.

He wears animal-skin boots and kilt and a heavy woolen or bearskin shirt. He has gloves and a belt of gold. The belt doubles his strength; the gloves help him control his hammer, Mjollnir.

The hammer itself is made of gold and is shaped like a sledgehammer. It has a ring of gold at the base of the handle and the handle itself is very short.

Individual Strokes: Begin the carving of this rune at its center, where the middle diagonal meets the vertical. Carve the diagonal up and to the right. Then carve the vertical stroke downward. Then carve the highest diagonal upward and to the left, reaching the top of the rune. Finally, carve the lowest diagonal up and to the left, returning to the center of the rune.

Color the rune in reverse order and direction to the carving. Start with the center and color downward and right. Then carve the topmost diagonal down and to the right. Then the vertical stroke is colored upward, and the middle diagonal is carved down and left into the center of the rune.

In both coloring and carving it is the center of the rune, its gateway position, which controls the carving. The only exception is the top of the rune, which is its power position. That diagonal cannot fall to the center, but the direction of its carving or coloring mirrors that of the one which does reach the center.

In carving, the rune emerges from the center; in coloring, it progresses inward to it.

When carving or coloring, recite:

> *For I shall take a journey*
> *on a horse no man can ride.*
> *It has eight legs*
> *and bears the dead.*

ᚠᚢᚦᚨᚱᚲᚷᚹᚺᚾᛁᛇᛃ�ᛋᛏᛒᛖᛗᛚᛜᚠᚢᚦᚱᚲᚷᚹᚺᚾᛁᛇᛃᛋᛏᛒ

Name: Ken

Phonetic Value: K

Aett: Freyja

Number: 6 in aett 1

Color: Yellow

Source: The Greek letter kappa, the Roman K

Image: A lit torch, particularly a torch in a cave with the wall reflecting the light. An initiation by torchlight, or one member of a torchlight parade.

Esoteric Meaning: Harnessed power; human beings tapping a power greater than their own. The power of light.

Magical Uses: Ken is useful for spiritual understanding, initiation, and guardianship. It can be used to bring strength to an individual, or for the banishment of dark forces of any kind. It can help overcome obstacles through learning. It is also a good luck charm. It is not, however, any good for combat. It banishes the dark; it doesn't defeat it.

Associated God: Kvasir or Mimir.

These two gods are different versions of the same concept. Mimir is the god who lives by the well of wisdom and guards it. But he is also said to be the severed head of the god of the same name. Killed by the Vanir, this god's head was preserved by Odin with herbs and kept by the well of inspiration. Because of Odin's magic Mimir's head could still speak, and gave sage advice.

Kvasir has two different explanations for his existence. In one he is simply one of the Vanir, the fertility gods, and as such is called the wisest of all gods.

In the other he is created from the saliva of the gods, Vanir and Aesir, and is an extremely wise mortal. In this it should be noted that saliva was a primitive means of causing fermentation, and served as the basis of oaths.

In the story, Kvasir was made as an oath of truce between the two groups of gods. He then went forth and used his wisdom to help others. Kvasir was murdered, and from his blood was made a mead which inspired wisdom in those who drank it.

In all cases, it is the same god of wisdom celebrated in words and drink.

Individual Strokes: Carve from the top down and left, then down and right. Carve the upper diagonal up and right, then the lower diagonal down and right. When carving or coloring, say:

I hold the light.

ᚠᚢᚦᚨᚱᚲᚷᚹᚺᚾᛁᛃᛇᛈᛉᛋᛏᛒᛖᛗᛚᛜᛞᛟᚠᚢᚦᚨᚱᚲᚷᚹᚺᚾᛁᛃᛇᛈᛉᛋᛏᛒ

Name: Gyfu

Phonetic Value: hard G

Aett: Freyja

Number: 7 in aett 1

Color: Red

Source: The Greek xi, Roman X, the Hallristing carving—X

Image: A cross, not to be confused with a cross of crucifixion, but the cross as an ancient pagan symbol.

Esoteric Meaning: Sacrifice and the ecological nature of pagan and especially runic magic. "A gift demands a gift," as the Norse saying goes; every decision requires the acceptance of one thing and the sacrifice of another.

Of Odin's eighteen runes, the last is secret. It could be the secret of sacrifice.

Magical Uses: Propitiation; removal of a curse (or karmic debt) through a sacrifice which brings with it right intention and action. A sign under which gifts can be made to the gods.

Associated God: Hod or Hoder.

Hod was the blind god who killed Balder. Depending on the source you trust, there are two causes for this: it may have been due to the trickery of Loki; alternatively, Hoder and Balder were brothers who came to fight over a woman, resulting in the death of Balder. In the later version Balder and Hoder are heroes rather than gods.

In either case (and there's a surprising amount of agreement between the two traditions), Hoder represents both blind fate and the agency of sacrifice.

Individual Strokes: To carve, start at the upper right corner and go down and to the left. Then start at the lower right and carve up and to the left.

Color from the upper right and go downward to the left. Then start at the upper left and color downward to the right.

In both cases we have an exchange—a gift demands a gift. The carving is on one level; the coloring is between levels.

ᛗᚼᛚᚱᛗᚠᚾᚦᚱᚱᚲᚷᚹᚺᛁᛁᚲᚴᚲᚤᛊᛏᛒᛗᛗᛚᚱᛗᚠᚾᚦᚱᚱᚲᚷᚹᚺᛁᛁᚲᚴ

This is one case in which what you say is different when carving and coloring. When carving, say:

> *A gift*
> *demands a gift.*

When coloring, say:

> *As I demand*
> *so I provide.*

ᚠᚢᚦᚨᚱᚲᚷᚹᚺᚾᛁᛃᛇᛋᛏᚤᛊᛒᛗᛖᛚᛜᛞᚠᚢᚦᚨᚱᚲᚷᚹᚺᚾᛁᛃᛇᛋᛏᚤᛒ

Name: Wynn

Phonetic Value: W

Aett: Freyja

Number: 8 in aett 1

Color: Blue

Source: Hallristing carving—↑

Image: Possibly a stylization of a snake being flayed. Odin was said to have some "glory wands" with which he struck a snake, causing the snake to fall into nine pieces. The name of the rune means "glory," and the glory wands may have been a divinatory method. Nine is a common number in Germanic paganism: remember Odin was the ninth creature created among the nine worlds.

Esoteric Meaning: Untapped power; glory in the sense of a divine power, which with a sudden move changes the affairs of mere mortals.

Magical Uses: Gaining the favor of superiors, whether mortal or immortal; obtaining promotion or passing tests. It is also useful for gaining wisdom, and is very useful for timing spell results.

If you want a spell to work at a particular time, wynn can be used to control the release of spell energy. So a talisman might use wynn to be made to work for nine days, in nine days, or some similar feature. Our method of measuring time (e.g., four o'clock on Thursday) is not suitable, and the rune works at its best with a multiple of nine.

Associated God: Skirnir.

Skirnir ("shining") was the messenger for Freyer to the goddess Gerd. He wooed her with presents and finally overcame her resistance with threats. The analogy is to a frozen field which eventually yields to the full force of the sun. The ice melts and the field can be tilled.

Skirnir should be visualized as a shining young man on a galloping horse. He bears a sword in its scabbard and on a shield he has nine golden apples.

Individual Strokes: Start with the vertical, carving downward. Then carve the diagonal downward and to the right. Then carve downward and to the left.

To color the rune, start at the top and color downward and right along the diagonal. The come back with the lower stroke to the left to reach the intersection with the vertical. Color the vertical itself last from bottom to top.

In carving and coloring we begin from the point of power. In other words, the implication of the rune—power from a higher source—is shown in the carving of the rune. In carving, everything comes from that source; in coloring, there is also repayment. Once the two diagonals are carved, which is the force establishing the structure, then return to the source is required.

When carving or coloring, recite the following:

> *The glories are many*
> *if you follow the path*
> *unto its end.*

ᚠᚢᚦᚨᚱᚲᚷᚹᚺᚾᛁᛃᛇᛈᛉᛊᛏᛒᛖᛗᛚᛜᛞᚠᚢᚦᚨᚱᚲᚷᚹᚺᚾᛁᛃᛇᛈᛉᛊᛏᛒ

Name: Hoel

Phonetic Value: H, though with more voice than in English

Aett: Heimdall

Number: 1 in aett 2

Color: White (or gray on a white background)

Source: The Greek eta or the Roman H

Image: Frost, ice, hail, winter weather generally.

Esoteric Meaning: Frost, ice, and cold as weapons of the frost giants. They are forces inimical to human survival, and also the lower impulses in ourselves. This is the rune of self-undoing and overcoming the tendency to undo one's own efforts.

Magical Uses: This is a rune of meditation and the council of silence, and aids consideration, decision, and meditation. It is also useful for overcoming aspects of our lower nature, including prankishness or bad habits. It is therefore very useful in overcoming impediments or obstacles to success.

Associated God: Heimdall.

Heimdall, a god of watchfulness and solitude, is the enemy of Loki, a mischief-maker. Heimdall is also the watchman who will warn others of the impending doom of Ragnarok.

He is a tall man with broad shoulders, swarthy skin, and naturally black hair which has been bleached by the sun. His hair and beard are unkempt, and his skin is leathery from living outdoors. His expression is kindly and smiling.

He wears a linen shirt and breeches, and a sealskin vest and shoes. All his clothes are well worn. He has a silver arm ring on his right arm and a gold one on the left. In his right hand is a ram's horn; in his left, a sword. The horn is the Gjallarhorn, with which he will warn of the coming Ragnarok.

Individual Strokes: Carve the right-hand vertical from the top down, then the diagonal upward and left; finally, the left-hand vertical is carved upward.

To color the rune, do the diagonal down and to the right, then the left vertical bottom to top, then the right vertical in the same direction.

Thus in carving we have the spiral inward of silence, concluding at the point of power. In coloring we see inner mischief and difficulties rising, but the downward coloring of the diagonal blunts their power.

For this rune, recite:

> *Ice and hail*
> *are my enemies*
> *without fail.*

ᚠᚢᚦᚨᚱᚲᚷᚹᚺᚾᛁ᛫ᛃᛈᛇᛉᛊᛏᛒᛖᛗᛚᛜᛞᛟᚠᚢᚦᚨᚱᚲᚷᚹᚺᚾᛁ᛫ᛃᛈᛇᛉᛊᛏᛒ

Name: Nyd
Phonetic Value: N
Aett: Heimdall
Number: 2 in aett 2
Color: Blue
Source: The Latin N, the Hallristing carving—+
Image: Unknown.

Esoteric Meaning: Harness internal power. The ability to achieve, as with a sudden rush of adrenalin or the creation of momentum such as is seen in business or election campaigns.

Magical Uses: Nyd is a widely useful rune, suitable for all forms of success and all types of achievement. However, remember that a gift demands a gift, and take note of the associated god.

The fourth of Odin's runes frees one from locks and fetters, which ties in well with the meaning of nyd.

Associated God: Norns.

Urd, Verdthandi, and Skuld are the three Norns, the fates of Germanic paganism. They are three old women wearing cloaks and hoods of purple. Two of the three bear staffs.

There is a certain element of fatalism here: we achieve what we are meant to achieve. If we are fated to accomplish something, we will do so, no matter how impossible it seems. On the other hand, if we are fated not to achieve something, then it will never come to us. But in a contradictory way, we create our own fates.

Individual Strokes: Carve the vertical straight down, then the diagonal left to right. Color the diagonal left to right, then the vertical from top to bottom. In both cases the position of power controls the situation: all force is emerging downward.

When carving the rune, say:

> *What I need,*
> *I achieve.*

When coloring nyd, recite:

> *I've got the power;*
> *I achieve.*

Name: Isa

Phonetic Value: I

Aett: Heimdall

Number: 3 in aett 2

Color: Black

Source: The Greek iota, the Roman I

Image: A spear; alternatively an icicle of great length, or even a staff.

Esoteric Meaning: The spear is one of the great weapons of Western magic, and was the favored weapon of Odin and Tiwaz. As a shaman, Odin carried a blackthorn staff.

In all these forms the spear is a symbol of masculinity (as opposed to the cup, which is feminine), of authority, delineation, and circumcision. We speak of the large spear-sized icicle of the north. This represents a circumcision of action through the weather, but that weather is viewed as if it were an entity in itself.

Magical Uses: Anything to do with authority. It is also good for dealing with conflict, and for magically gathering allies (who must be your equals, or nearly so). It can also uncover enemies.

Associated God: Skadi.

Skadi was a frost giant associated with skiing and hunting. She is in some ways an equivalent to the Roman Diana in that she is a woman in youth. She is not a lunar deity, but a winter goddess (or giantess) who is helpful to humankind.

Individual Strokes: Carve up; color down. The dominant and subordinate positions are in contention. Recite:

My spear flies true.

Name: Ger

Phonetic Value: Y, as in yacht. The name has nothing to do with the phonetic value

Aett: Heimdall

Number: 4 in aett 2

Color: Brown

Source: Hallristing carving of the swastika—

Image: Annual harvest, the year. In primitive times, the year meant the harvest year and the harvest festival which marked the change. It is a symbol of community and festival, togetherness and happiness.

It is also a symbol of right thoughts and right action leading to right results. Where nyd is sudden action leading to success, ger shows the culmination of efforts over a long period of time, and is a much quieter operation.

Magical Uses: Comfort; harmony with others. It is also good for gardening, farming, having a happy home, and good times. Put ger over the door of your house on New Year's Eve. Use indelible ink because the luck is meant to last as long as ger remains there.

Associated God: Saga.

Saga was the goddess who drank with Odin every day. She is a goddess of harvest and household pleasures. It is possible that another form of her was Sif, Thor's wife.

Individual Strokes: Start at the top of the uppermost diagonal and carve down and to the right. The carve the lowest diagonal up and to the left. Next carve the central diagonals down and right, then up and right.

The position of power is muted in this rune. The carving shows the influence of seasons bringing order to otherwise independent forces. The coloring shows the lower controlling the power, just as a farmer makes use of the seasons to grow crops. We cannot change fundamental law, but if we use it properly it benefits us.

The words for carving and coloring are:

Harvest time
and planting time
the crop is cared for
and made to grow.

Name: Eoh
Phonetic Value: Between an E and an I
Aett: Heimdall
Number: 5 in aett 2
Color: Green
Source: Hallristing carving— ᚼ

Image: A yew, which is a form of fir tree. The tree was sacred to runecraft, and traditionally the runes were carved into pieces of yew or, as Odin's poem puts it, into the root of a sapling.

Esoteric Meaning: As hermaphrodites and conifers the trees symbolized immortality. That they remained green in winter aided this association, as did the fact that the needles are poisonous. This implies that mortal beings are refused immortality.

This rune reminds us that it is better not to pledge at all than to pledge overmuch, since this rune is a symbol of the limits of life. It is a symbol of the definition of our lives.

Of the runes in Odin's poem, the fifth is one to stop an arrow in flight, no matter how swiftly it travels. The fixing of it echoes the set boundaries of eoh.

Magical Uses: Protection of oneself and one's rights. When things are out of kilter this rune can help set them back in line. However, if it is the runecaster who is out of whack, things suffer for it. The rune can thus be used in conjunction with other runes to keep the magic of the whole within reasonable bounds. It forms a kind of feedback mechanism within talismans and rune magic.

Associated God: Forseti, the god of justice.

Little is known of Forseti, and even what is known is often disputed, but his function is clear. Forseti was a son of Balder who stilled strife and settled disputes.

He is associated with a group of twelve, with himself as thirteenth or leader. Some have said this was in imitation of Christianity, but the idea of a council of twelve with a leader emerges elsewhere in Nordic myths, and is also present in paganism in general.

He is associated with a sacred spring from which water must be drawn in silence. (There was such a spring in Fotise-land, an island near Denmark. St. Willebrod baptized three men in it and killed a cow there to defile it.) Forseti also appears with a golden axe that can make springs well up from the earth.

Forseti should be visualized in Glitnir, his hall of gold and silver. You should visualize yourself approaching it from a spring in the wilderness. The hall itself is set in the wilderness and is not protected by walls.

He carries a light, twin-bladed axe made of gold. This axe has a long handle, but is too light to be used as a weapon.

Forseti himself is a very tall man of grave countenance. He rarely speaks. He has gray eyes and long, blond hair which is often tied into a ponytail in the back; a woolly beard and mustache cover his face. His eyes are keen and penetrating.

He wears soft gray linen clothing decorated with filigreed gold and leather, and soft leather boots.

Individual Strokes: To carve eoh, begin by doing the upper diagonal down and to the right, then the central vertical down. The lower diagonal is then carved down and to the right.

When coloring, we basically reverse the system. Start with the lower diagonal and color up and to the left. Then color the central vertical straight up, and finish with the upper diagonal down and to the right.

The words to recite for each line are:

> *Though poisonous the fruit,*
> *immortal is the promise*
> *of the sacred tree.*

ᚠᚢᚦᚨᚱᚲᚷᚹᚺᚾᛁ᛬ᛃᛈᛇᛦᛋᛏᛒᛖᛗᛚᛜᛞᚠᚢᚦᚨᚱᚲᚷᚹᚺᚾᛁ᛬ᛃᛈᛇᛦᛋᛏᛒ

Name: Poerdh

Phonetic Value: P

Aett: Heimdall

Number: 6 in aett 2

Color: Red

Source: The Greek letter sigma or Hallristing carving—

Image: A burial mound and its entrance. Offerings were often made to various gods (including Freyer) by leaving objects in a burial mound. Although we have the delightful image of friends talking within the mound, there are also the *draugr*, vampire-like creatures who rose from the dead to prey on the living. The name "draugr" is a version of "follower of the lie."

Esoteric Meaning: The final boundary of human life. Not the journey of rad from which return is possible, but the finality of death, the feeling of loss, and the understanding that what is now will someday not be.

In Odin's poem the twelfth rune will, when carved and colored, let a dead person speak.

Magical Uses: It opens or provides a barrier to the dark forces including the realms of the dead. It confronts us with our weaknesses, our failures, and our regrets. It makes us deal with the question of what we would do if we died now. It is therefore a useful rune of test and attack.

Associated God: Loki.

Invocation of Loki would only be good for theft, lies, destruction, death, and pain. He is the bound giant underground.

Individual Strokes: Carve the vertical stroke from top to bottom, then carve the lower inner diagonal up and right. Then the outer upper diagonal is carved up and right, followed by the lower outer diagonal down and right. Finally, the upper inner diagonal is carved down and right.

To color the rune, follow the lines around. Start with the upper outer diagonal: color this left and down. Then do the inner upper diagonal up and left. Then color the vertical straight down, so the whole looks a little like a flag on a pole. Next color the inner diagonal up and right, then the outer lower diagonal down and right.

In this the carving has no natural order—all forces are left to contend against each other. In coloring, though it looks ordered, magically it is only a boundary without reference to power coming down or rising up.

With the carving and coloring, this is what you must say:

> *Death*
> *is a journey*
> *and a change*
> *that always leads*
> *to new life.*

Uniquely, the words do not simply reinforce the message of the rune, but also seek to keep its power within bounds.

ᚠᚢᚦᚫᚱᚲᚷᚹᚺᚾᛁᛃᛇᛈᛉᛊᛏᛒᛗᛚᛜᛞᚠᚢᚦᚫᚱᚲᚷᚹᚺᚾᛁᛃᛇᛊᛏᛒ

Name: Eohl

Phonetic Value: Z (Like ger, the name has nothing to do with the phonetic value)

Aett: Heimdall

Number: 7 in aett 2

Color: Purple

Source: Hallristing carving—

Image: A magic wand. In Germanic paganism the end of the wand pointed at people or objects was often splayed into two or three branches. Can also be a splayed hand or an elk's horn. It has been suggested to be an elk's head about to butt, which would make it rather like ur.

Esoteric Meaning: Protection and defense of all kinds at all times, physical or spiritual, personal or collective.

Of Odin's eighteen runes, the third blunts an enemy's sword or softens his staff so he cannot harm.

Magical Uses: Any possible form of protection from every possible source of danger is eohl's domain.

Associated God: Magni and Modi.

They are the sons of Thor—their names translate as Might and Wrath—and will inherit from their father the hammer Mjollnir. They are red-haired, like their father. They each wear one metal glove (Magni the right, Modi the left). They wear animal skins for clothes.

Individual Strokes: Carve the vertical down, then the left diagonal up and left, then the right diagonal up and right.

Coloring starts with the vertical up, then the left diagonal down, then the right diagonal down.

The carving indicates the seeking of power from higher forces; the coloring, the bringing of all things to the point of becoming. In this way all externals are locked out.

During carving and coloring, say:

> *By my sword*
> *and by my magic*
> *I am defended.*

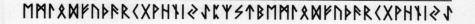

Name: Sighel

Phonetic Value: S

Aett: Heimdall

Number: 8 in aett 2

Source: The Roman S. Hallristing symbols of the sun, including the swastika and sunwheel

Image: The sun and all symbols of the sun.

Esoteric Meaning: In its various forms, the sun is a symbol of personal, transcendent salvation. This is true whether we are talking about pagans of the Germanic tribes or those of Rome, Persia, or India.

In Germanic paganism the world might end with Ragnarok, but it would be reborn. The transcendence would occur, and this promise is encompassed in sighel.

The tenth of Odin's runes sends witches "in a spin" and does not let them make their way back to their doors by sunrise.

Magical Uses: Transcendent power, salvation, knowledge, strength in times of trouble. Also useful for matters of success and divination. Will counter all dark forces.

Associated God: Vor, the All-Seeing.

Vor was the goddess from whom nothing could be hidden.

Individual Strokes: This is the only rune in which carving and coloring strokes are exactly the same. Start at the top of the rune and carve down, then the middle diagonal up and right, then the lowest diagonal down and left.

In this you represent the power from above being brought down, not as an imposition (as with nyd) but as a structuring force.

For carving and coloring, say:

> *Sun and wind*
> *light of day*
> *will perfect the world again.*

Name: Tyr
Phonetic Value: T
Aett: Tir
Number: 1 in aett 3
Color: Red
Source: Hallristing carving—↑
Image: The world tree or the pillar which holds up the sky. Can also be a spear.

Esoteric Meaning: Tyr was a rune often painted on pagan shields to give their bearers more courage and to protect the warriors in battle. It also appears as a single rune on a number of swords and daggers.

It stands not only for the spear but also for the pillar that holds up the sky. This was a form of an ancient belief which shows up as a pillar in some cultures, or as the world tree Yggdrasil, or as a mountain as in Persia. The pillar stood for the natural order of things. It was the power that made things distinct and kept them as they are.

The sacred pillar was not only associated with Tiwaz in his form of sky-god (before the cult of Odin ousted him); in the German assembly (the *thing*) the pillar was commonly represented by a physical pillar and oaths could be taken on it. In the cult of Thor, too, the pillar had a part to play.

Magical Uses: A symbol of divine protection, of justice and honor in war or duel. It can be used to defend against or attack known enemies. It ensures victory and the righting of injustice, and can be used to bind an oath.

Associated God: Tiwaz or Tir.

Tiwaz is the older name, harkening to the god when he was supreme in the Norse pantheon just as Zeus was in the Greek. The names of the two gods come from the same source—*dayus*, meaning "day." Tir is a late pagan war god, and it is only recently we've noted how old the deity really is. Rock carvings from the Bronze Age show a one-handed god. He is the god of contract, a god of the oath as well as the god of justice and war.

Tir should be visualized as a tall man, with blond braided hair and blue eyes. His right hand is missing and has not been capped, so the stump still shows the toothmarks of the wolf Fenrir.

He wears a metal helmet which bears horns or falcon wings. He wears a black leather eyepatch over his right eye. He has on a black (or sometimes brown) leather jerkin with some rings (not many) sewn onto it. He has a plain scabbard worn on his right; the sword is in his left hand.

He wears brown trousers of woven cloth, black boots set with metal rings, and has a cloak of wolfskin. The head of one of the wolves hangs over one shoulder.

Individual Strokes: Tyr is carved from the point of power. Carve the left diagonal, the vertical, then the right diagonal. All strokes should be made downward.

Color the vertical downward, the left diagonal downward, then the right diagonal downward.

Divine justice is imposed from the point of power, but the exact means by which it is imposed differs. This is the message of the strokes.

When carving or coloring, say:

> *Vault of the sky,*
> *justice and power,*
> *I defend thee.*

Name: Boerc

Phonetic Value: B

Aett: Tir

Number: 2 in aett 3

Color: Blue

Source: The Greek beta, the Roman B

Image: A bundle of birch rods held with a leather strap.

Esoteric Meaning: Birch rods had special uses in pagan times. They were used to flagellate, which was supposed to heal, to keep someone healthy, and to grant fertility to women who wanted to become pregnant or to men who wanted to impregnate a woman. Birch rods were often set at the woman's bed when she gave birth, to ease the process.

They were also used for atonement. The use of birch rods didn't really die out until this century. It may have been harsher than fines or jail, but at the end of it everyone, including the wrong-doer, could say atonement had been given.

Magical Uses: Healing, good health, calming troubled minds, childbirth and fertility.

Associated God: Idun.

Idun was the goddess who tended the apples of immortality for the gods.

Individual Strokes: Carve the uppermost diagonal down and right. Then carve the diagonal second from the bottom from where it meets the vertical down and to the right. Next carve the vertical stroke upward. The rune should now look something like os. Now carve the lowest diagonal from the base up and right. Finally, carve the diagonal from the center of the rune up and right, so it will meet the topmost vertical.

To color, start with the vertical from the bottom up. Then (coloring always to the right) do the diagonals: lowest, second lowest, second highest, highest.

In carving, the power comes from above and the diagonals respond by changing (they emerge from the center, which is the place of becoming). In coloring, the attempt is made to return to the source of power. First contact is made by the vertical and then in step fashion the diagonals, through exchange, provide for the return.

When carving boerc, keep the mind blank. When coloring, say:

Life eternal,
fertility,
freedom and joy
are provided
to initiates.

ᚠᚢᚦᚨᚱᚲᚷᚹᚺᚾᛁ⟨ᛃᛇᛏᛦᛋᛏᛒᛗᛗᛚᚷᛞᚠᚢᚦᚨᚱᚲᚷᚹᚺᚾᛁ⟨ᛃᛚᚷᛦᛋᛏᛒ

Name: Ehwis

Phonetic Value: Short E

Aett: Tir

Number: 3 in aett 3

Color: White

Source: The Greek mu, the Roman M, or a symbol similar to that used by the Spartans in the worship of Castor and Pollux. Also the Hallristing rune—

Image: Two horsemen, their horses at full gallop, grasp each other's arms. Also the heads of two horses facing one another. There is a theory that the rune represents two beams held by a crossbeam (like a modern door) or a primitive bellows. Fire was part of the rituals of several pagan sects.

Esoteric Meaning: The meaning of this rune is bound with its associated god (or gods), the Aclis.

In the poem of Odin, the seventh rune puts out fires of a friend's house.

Magical Uses: A call for divine aid in times of trouble, gathering of bonds of friendship, and the protection of friends. It can call aid from unlooked-for places. It is also a general good luck charm.

Associated God: The Aclis, Germanic twin gods.

We learn about the Aclis from Tacitus, who was surprised at their similarity to the Greek Castor and Pollux. They were the sons of the sky-god; in this case, probably Tiwaz rather than Odin. They were noted horsemen, and horse races were central to their cult—ehwis derives from the same word as horse.

A number of royal houses traced their ancestry back to brothers who shared kingship. In some of these ancestries, like the myth of the Aclis, one brother killed the other. A form of this myth, I believe, can be found in the myth of Hoder killing Balder.

Worship of the Aclis involved horse races, but the riders raced joined in pairs. Their priests were "dressed like women," or so Tacitus tells us. He also said there was no image used in the religion.

Individual Strokes: Carve the left diagonal down and right, then the right diagonal up and right. Carve first the left then the right vertical down.

Color the right vertical up, then the left vertical down. Color the right diagonal then the left diagonal from left to right, heading down and finishing in the middle of the rune.

The carving indicates the two Aclis in life. The color shows them after one has died (one colored up, the other down). In both cases the diagonals meet at the point of becoming, showing the response to their own destinies.

When carving or coloring, say:

> *Far and wide*
> *the brothers roam*
> *to aid those*
> *who seek their help.*

ᚠᚢᚦᚨᚱᚲᚷᚹᚺᚾᛁᛇᛃᛈᛣᛊᛏᛒᛖᛗᛚᛜᚢᚦᚨᚱᚲᚷᚹᚺᚾᛁᛇᛃᛈᛣᛊᛏᛒ

Name: Manu

Phonetic Value: M

Aett: Tir

Number: 4 in aett 3

Color: Purple

Source: The Greek mu, the Hallristing carving— ⋈

Image: A human being: gender and race are irrelevant to the meaning of the rune.

Esoteric Meaning: Manu is the human being: an individual or the species as a whole. It is not a tribal orientation of us-them. It is therefore not a racial description at all. A black woman is as much a part of this rune as is a male of Germanic descent.

In being human, manu describes us as having an essential role in the universe, although we are not the center of the universe. The gods are as important as we are (more so, in fact) and have a role we cannot fulfill—something scientific materialism keeps proving but not admitting.

Magical Uses: Manu helps in knowing oneself. It can therefore be used in meditation (see Chapter 3), to increase dreaming, or to enhance the truth of dreams. It can be used in conjunction with other runes to personalize matters or magic for or on a particular individual. It is also useful for cleansing oneself, a ritual which makes the afterlife more pleasant.

In Odin's poem of runes, the second is one that must be learned by anyone who hopes to be a healer. Without knowing the patient, no healing is possible.

Associated God: Njord, the Sea-God.

Njord is one of the Vanir, the fertility gods. He is the fruitfulness of the sea, though he, like all sea deities, has a dark side.

He is a blond-haired man. His hair and beard lie in tangles, and his beard reaches his waist. He has a great deal of body hair and leathery skin, and is covered with scars. He has a laughing expression and kind eyes that carry a hint of sadness.

He wears neither shirt nor shoes, merely grey canvas breeches held up by a rope. On his left arm is a silver arm ring carved with runes. On his head is a fillet of leather.

He carries a hook in one hand and a net in the other. The net trails after him. That hand (his left) is missing a couple of finger joints.

Individual Strokes: Carve the left then the right vertical upward. Then the diagonals downward and to the right, then downward and to the left.

Color the diagonals, first downward and to the right, then downward and to the left. Do the left vertical upward, then the right vertical downward.

Here the point of becoming (the middle) can change just as humans can change their goals in and attitudes toward life.

Carving begins with supplication—carving the verticals up. From the supplication comes structure, as seen in the diagonals. In this we see something like a child learning to structure his or her self and world.

In coloring, the diagonals come first, showing an exchange beween equals. The verticals are then carved, one up and one down, showing the exchange to be guided by the structure already existing. In this, think of adults as children in comparison to the gods.

When carving, recite the following:

> *With my gods*
> *by my sword*
> *with my harvest*
> *I live.*

When coloring, recite:

> *From birth*
> *to grave,*
> *I live by justice*
> *and my oath.*

ᚠᚢᚦᚨᚱᚲᚷᚹᚺᚾᛁᛃᛇᛈᛉᛊᛏᛒᛖᛗᛚᛜᛞᚠᚢᚦᚨᚱᚲᚷᚹᚺᚾᛁᛃᛇᛈᛉᛊᛏᛒ

Name: Lagu

Phonetic Value: L

Aett: Tir

Number: 5 in aett 3

Color: Green

Source: Hallristing carving—↑

Image: A wave breaking the shore seen at eye level from the side.

Esoteric Meaning: A symbol of water. Water is life to us all, but as any seafaring people know, it can be our death. Water is also transition. Pagans of the Germanic tribes splashed water on their newborns; they used beer as the oath from the individual to members of a group. (Remember that beer was fermented by spitting in it. It therefore proved a perfect means of building an oath.) They saw men drown. Lagu is thus a symbol of transition between states: birth, binding oath, and death.

Associated God: Aegir and Ran.

Aegir and his wife Ran were sea deities. They had an underwater court and were excellent brewers. But they had a dark side. The sea was called the "jaws of Aegir," and Ran was said to drag men under the sea with a net.

Individual Strokes: Carve down—first the vertical, then the diagonal. Color the vertical up, then the diagonal down.

The carving shows the imposition of power by the implacable sea; the coloring, the seeking and receiving of the sea's power.

For each stroke, recite one line of the following:

> *Life grows,*
> *life goes on.*

Name: Ing

Phonetic Value: Ng as in thing

Aett: Tir

Number: 6 of aett 3

Color: Black

Source: The Roman D

Image: A compound of houses behind a wall of standing logs.

Esoteric Meaning: The name is taken to mean "the people," and sometimes specifically the Danish people. But the name also refers to a god of the earth who preceded Tiwaz, who himself preceded Odin.

It refers to the concept of community, of people living and working together.

Magical Uses: To gather people or to influence them. It can be used to establish dedication and loyalty, the "we" of a group. It can be used as a rune of fascination, which makes it suitable for strengthening hypnosis, trance, or meditation. It can also be used for gaining the respect of others, or gaining influential positions in a community.

Associated God: Freyer.

Freyer is the twin of the goddess Freyja. He is a fertility god of peace, joy, and plenty, though his protection was also sought in war. He oversaw many of the essential aspects of community, such as good harvests, providing children to families, and sanctioning marriages. He was the patron of festivals, charity, and community activities apart from politics.

He should be visualized as a man in his forties, lithe of stature, and fit. He has red hair and a beard. He wears a sleeveless white woolen jerkin, breeches, and boots. He wears a silver arm ring, a black leather belt, and an empty scabbard.

Individual Strokes: Carve the right side first, going first down and right, then down and left. Then the strokes on the left are carved, first down and left, then down and right.

Color the left side first: down and left, then down and right. Then the right side: down and right, then down and left.

All strokes are downward because the existence and running of community is set by divine law. But the strokes show how the law is felt by the greatest and the least and that the lesser (human) imitates the greater (divine), though in a different fashion.

When carving or coloring, recite:

My people
who support me
I shall support
by right action.

ᛗᛖᛚᛉᛗᚠᚾᚦᚨᚱᚲᚷᚹᚺᚾᛁᚴ ᛋᛚᚲᚤᛏᛒᛗᛗᛚᛉᛗᚠᚾᚦᚨᚱᚲᚷᚹᚺᛁᚴᛋ

Name: Odel

Phonetic Value: O, particularly the long O

Aett: Tir

Number: 7 in aett 3

Color: Brown

Source: Unknown. Several Hallristing carvings, if taken together, might give the rune, but none singly. Odel may be modeled on the shape of Ing, a possibility suggested by their similar meanings

Image: Possibly a lock.

Esoteric Meaning: Odel refers to property and goods, inheritance, name, and reputation. Family was much more important in pagan society than in our own. While divorce (and more commonly, orphanage) existed, it did not mean the child was cut off from grandparents or aunts and uncles. Children in each family were taught a kind of familial mythology which extolled their ancestors.

In Odin's poem, the seventeenth rune is a charm that will make a girl loathe to leave him; that is, it draws her into a commitment.

Magical Uses: To call on ancestral powers, including calling up their spirits. This is a rune of merchants, but also the land-holding nobles—both classes in which inheritance played a key role.

It thus aids in partnerships, whether those of business, politics, or marriage. It can be used to guard family fortunes or build the strength of a dynasty.

It can also develop strengths and talents in an individual. These abilities are considered latent, and brought out by reference to ancestral (or genetic) potential.

Associated God: Var.

Var was the goddess invoked for marriage, for she heard the marriage vows and punished transgressors.

Individual Strokes: Start at the lower left, carving up and to the right. Then cross over and carve down and right, giving a figure of an X, rather like gyfu. Next carve from the point of power down and to the right, then the last diagonal down and left.

To color, start at the lower left and color up and right. Continue by coloring up and left. It should now look like a backward and slightly lopsided ken. Then from the lower right-hand point color up and left, then turn and color up and right.

In carving, the power joins an established structure, just as the extended family joins in the love of the couple. In coloring, the influence of exchange reaches back to the point of power as the new link in the chain is established.

The lines to recite here are:

My ancestors,
my self,
my children,
the rope is unbroken.

ᛖᛗᛚ ᚨᛗᚠᚢᚦᚨᚱᚲᚷᚹᚺᚾᛁᚲ ᛋᚲᛉᛋᛏᛒᛖᛗᛚ ᚨᛗᚠᚢᚦᚨᚱᚲᚷᚹᚺᛁᚲᛋ

Name: Doerg

Phonetic Value: Between a d and a dth (the th being voiced like in father)

Aett: Tir

Number: 8 in aett 3

Color: Yellow

Source: Hallristing carving—ᛉ

Image: A cart pulled by shining horses, the wheel of which is the sun disc.

Esoteric Meaning: Day, daylight, the powers of light. But unlike the harnessed powers in the rune ken, these are powers which exceed true human control, structuring things by their own right. Unlike sighel, the powers here are essentially human-oriented.

A number of Germanic tribes worshiped a sun chariot. Models of these carts with wheels inlaid in gold still exist, and were undoubtedly models of full-sized carts used at festivals.

The first rune in Odin's poem is a charm that will give comfort in grief, lessen pain, and cure sickness.

Magical Uses: It is a good luck charm, and can also be used to advance one's station in life. It is helpful for spiritual advancement and understanding. It is an expression of universal love.

Associated God: Balder, the dying god.

The name Balder comes from a root word meaning "bright day." He is a deity of the sky, though not of war. He is a god of justice, wisdom, and mercy. He is a god of poetry, inspiration, and entertainments.

He should be seen as a young man not quite at full maturity, and either clean-shaven or lightly bearded. He has bright blue eyes and bright blond hair. He wears a tunic of yellow linen with a yellow belt. He wears gold arm rings and a yellow cap on his head and carries a golden battle axe.

Individual Strokes: Carve the left vertical down, then the diagonal up and right. Then the right vertical is carved down, then the diagonal down and right.

Color the left and then the right vertical down. Then the diagonals are colored from left to right, going first from bottom up and then top down.

In the carving and coloring the power from above creates the exchange of the diagonals: the power builds the structure through which we live. In carving, this is done piecemeal; in coloring, the whole is set before exchange commences. We are looking here at origin and maintenance of the divine laws.

In this rune alone, nothing is recited. The mind should be kept free of words. Perhaps silence in the light is a fitting concept with which to end the runes.

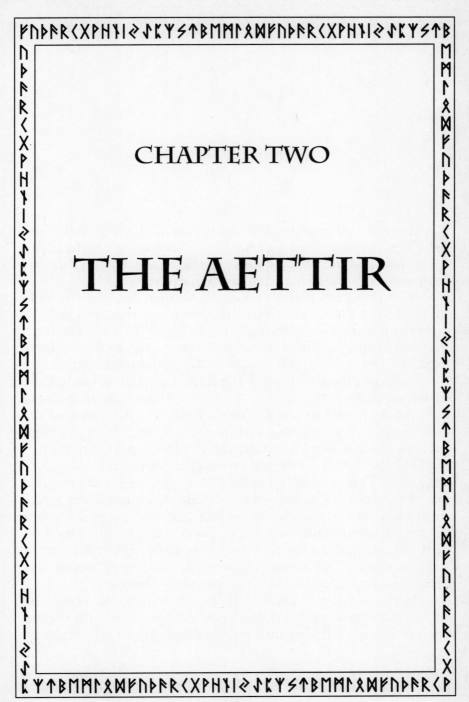

CHAPTER TWO

THE AETTIR

There are three aettir (aett is singular, aettir is plural) of the Elder Futhark. This fact has often been mentioned in both occult and academic books on the runes, but no one has bothered to wonder what this division means.

The Enochian alphabet has no similar division; its only internal structure is its alphabetic order and numerology. The Hebrew alphabet has both these divisions and the division between single, double, and mother letters. This last division was used by MacGregor Mathers to form his Rosicrucian symbol.

Perhaps this is why when the runes regained popularity the existence of the aettir did not excite much attention. Indeed, the only mention of their use was as the basis of ciphers such as the twig runes or tent runes. Additionally the aettir form the basis for runic numerology, a sophisticated subject in its own right.

But the aettir, on examination, create a careful division of the runes. This system has several implications for the magical use of the runes. The aettir not only imply an initiatory structure, each aett being one degree in a three-degree system, but they seem to reflect the age-old division of Aryan tribal society: nurturer, warrior, and priest/king. This theory of the division of Aryan societies, by the way, is not an occult theory, but an academic one associated most closely with G. Dumezil.

In its simplest form, the theory is as follows. When the Aryan tribes swept from the steppes, they brought with them a society already divided into three groupings, which might be called protocastes. The names of these groupings have already been mentioned.

These groupings affected the different Aryan societies in a variety of ways. In India the divisions multiplied, became more fixed, and were transformed into the caste system. In Iran, too, the caste developed but was much less complicated and rigid, and eventually atrophied into merely two divisions: priest/king and everybody else.

These divisions apparently explain a wide variety of phenomena. For example, in early Rome there were priesthoods called flamens. G. Dumezil believed the Latin *flamen* to be a corruption of "brahman."

Furthermore, there were three major and twelve minor such priesthoods—priesthood here being an office held by an individual. The three major priesthoods were dedicated to the gods Quiurnus, Mars, and Jupiter. Dumezil saw these as reflecting the nurturer, warrior, and priest/king respectively.

Similarly, medieval society with its division of people— "those who work, those who pray, and those who fight"— reflected the same ancient traditions. Dumezil saw the same division in Germanic society.

We should not think Dumezil's ideas have been universally accepted. He did not have an explanation, for example, why ancient Greece (meaning after the Dorian invasion) totally lacked these divisions. Certainly the flamenic priesthoods may have been named after the hat which identified them, as has been suggested. The volume of contentious voices certainly increases when we move from divisions in society to the images Dumezil said accompanied the tribes, in effect turning Jung's collective unconscious into an historical image in its own right.

What Dumezil has done, however, is trace structures of society to their common origin. Where we find the structure remaining in society we can expect it to exist in its institutions. This is certainly the case with the Germanic tribes.

The divisions Dumezil noted were essentially those of the Germanic pagans. They had nurturers in their farmers, women, and to an extent, merchants. They had their warriors, the Vikings being one example, and their priest/kings. Many royal houses traced their ancestry back to one of the gods. In the pagan era all royalty had divine sanction.

These divisions are reflected in the aettir of the runes in different ways. If you look carefully, you may notice some overlap in the duties of the runes. Each aett has its complement of functions and its own character.

FREYJA'S AETT

The first aett is Freyja's, the aett of the nurturer: the mother, the farmer, and the merchant. It is also the aettir of the first degree and shows this in its structure. The runes set three pairs of opposites which are fairly typical of the kind of test/choice early students face in initiatory training.

Take the first two letters: feoh and ur. These are domesticated and wild oxen, respectively. The similarity is obvious, since both deal with cattle. The distinction is between the social, domesticated, and responsible on one hand and the wild, untamed nature on the other.

Do not assume that feoh is good and ur is bad. The task of the student is as much to get away from his or her own conventional ways of thinking as to learn the methods of magic. On the other hand, the student must often face parts of him or herself he or she hoped never to face again: the student must learn to capture and tame the wild side of his or her own psyche.

The second pair, thorn and os, is even easier to see as a dichotomy, since it admits no ambiguity. It is all demons, especially the one called Thorn, versus all gods, especially Odin. In other words, the student has to choose the gods with every fiber of his or her being.

To choose the gods only because it is expected is not good enough. The student has to see the reality of the choice, and make it using all the factors of him or herself unleashed (the lesson of feoh and ur).

ᚠᚢᚦᚨᚱᚲᚷᚹᚺᚾᛁᛃᛇᛈᛉᛊᛏᛒᛖᛗᛚᛜᛞᚠᚢᚦᚨᚱᚲᚷᚹᚺᚾᛁᛃᛊᛁᛏᛒ

The third pair, rad and ken, complete the simple opposites in this aettir. They are the otherworld and the journey to the land of the dead on one hand, the light of the torch on the other.

With this pair we seem to have an image of a two-part initiation. On the physical level we have a person in a cave (rad) who has been subject to sensory deprivation (darkness) being brought the light (ken) before being brought out of the cave as if reborn.

Psychologically, we have a typical shamanic ride into the otherworld on a cart or an animal (rad). There the shaman uses his or her harnessed magical powers (ken) as a guide, conducts the journey safely, and returns.

Note that initiations in caves were common in both Germanic and Celtic cultures. In the case of the Germanic tribes, torches were a symbol of magical power. Even today torchlight parades, a tradition started by the pagans, take place.

The final two runes are gyfu and wynn. Gyfu is the gift, the exchange; wynn, the glory. In the light of previous pairs it would seem the parallel here is that in return for the gift the student receives the glory, which in this case means wisdom.

The sacrifices the student has made (and a last such sacrifice may be indicated by the rune gyfu) yield the wisdom of wynn. The student has passed the degree of the nurturer (Freyja) and it ready to undergo the tests of the warrior, Heimdall.

HEIMDALL'S AETT

Heimdall is sometimes thought of as a god of silence, which might seem like priestly meditation to some. I believe he, in conjunction with Loki, forms a special description of the world. Loki is the bound giant whose fingers eat away at coastlines.

Loki is a shapeshifter, as dunes change shape. He steals, as erosion steals topsoil or land. Yet he brings the gods their greatest treasures (usually of gold), as erosion reveals alluvial gold or other items.

Heimdall is the watcher against this. He is associated with goats because they live on the cliffs identified with him. He is identified with sea cliffs because they are seen as Heimdall watching for Loki's arrival. His horn is the waves crashing against the surf, the sound heard throughout the nine worlds.

He is associated with the land, in that *Heim*dall refers to the land just as do the names Vana*heim* and Svartalf*heim*. Similarly, Freyja is called *Mer*doll, which is the sea equivalent of *Heim*dall. But Heimdall himself was born of the sea, as land is often thought (correctly, geologically speaking) to be born of the sea.

In essence, Heimdall is a warrior. Ever-watchful, he struggles against overwhelming odds, showing unending courage in his watchfulness.

His aett begins with Hoel (all the aettir begin with the initial of the god of the aett). It is winter, ice, and the season of cold. In this we again have the dichotomy of Loki and Heimdall.

Winter is a season in which people spend long months indoors. Pranks and mischief become common and can go too far. This was the sort of thing against which Heimdall, watchful and patient, was to stand.

The second rune is nyd, necessity. Long periods of enforced rest, even boredom, can lead one past the obvious. The usual mechanisms of personality break down and the individual reaches for something inside him or herself. He or she finds sources of power beyond his or her dreams.

When such things occur, and they do occur in several societies, they are described in terms of combat or in relation to a warrior. It is interesting to note here that Freyja's aett starts with safety and moves to danger, while Heimdall's aett starts with danger and moves to its resolution.

The next two runes of Heimdall seem to repeat the relationship of the first two: isa (spear or ice) and ger (the year, especially the harvest). Naturally isa (as ice) parallels hoel, and ger (harvest with the implication of winter stores) parallels nyd.

If so, this implies the application of the power of nyd, in turn made necessary by hoel. Defense of the food stores against the enemy, human or natural, is part of this. But there is another dichotomy represented here.

ᚠᚢᚦᚨᚱᚲᚷᚹᚺᚾᛁᛇᛃᛚᚲᛉᛋᛏᛒᛖᛗᛚᛉᛗᚠᚢᚦᚨᚱᚲᚷᚹᚺᚾᛁᛇᛃᛚᚲᛉᛋᛏᛒ

Isa is the barren time of winter. Ger is the fruitfulness of the harvest. In this the warrior reaches into his or her lowermost depths to find the wellspring of personal strength, a strength which exists almost by natural law.

The runes go through boredom and find necessity. They go through barrenness and find fruitfulness. One would expect a third such division, yet the next two runes do not provide it.

Both eoh and poerdh deal with restriction. Eoh is natural restriction, and might be compared to the literal meaning of the Latin *prohibit*, which means "for life." Poerdh is the funeral mound and its entrance. It is death not in the mold of rad, a crossable state, but it is death as a warrior finds it—an impenetrable barrier; a final limit.

The last two runes are also similar in direction, but on different scales. That is, eohl is protection while sighel is the sun as salvation and protection.

Restriction is matched with protection and death is matched with salvation. In this poerdh is not an absolute barrier; any breach of that barrier exists only through a higher power. Sighel, as the sun, transcends death. It is not the warrior who digs permanently deeper into him or herself to eventually overcome even death: for this he or she requires outside aid. With that in mind, we turn to the third aettir.

TIR'S AETT

Tir, in his original form of Tiwaz, was the head of the Germanic pantheon. His name comes from the same source as Jupiter (originally Deus Pitar) and Zeus. He was a sky god whose worship went back at least to the Bronze Age; we have carvings which show a one-handed figure who is taken to be a god.

It is possible that his ancestry is much older than this. The rough outline of the Germanic mythic universe, a column or tree holding up a skull which is the sky, seems to go back to the days of the Neanderthal. In a Neanderthal cave, a stick on which rests a skull has been found. Surrounding the stick is a ring of stones. The stick relates to Yggdrasil, the world tree; the skull is the skull that is the sky. The stones can be compared to the Midgard serpent. The parallels are too close to ignore.

The first rune of the aettir is tyr, a complex rune that is not only its god's initial but also a version of his name. It is a rune that represents victory and protection and is a symbol of cosmic justice.

We in the modern world forget that among ancient tribes war was seen as a test, and the gods gave victory to those who were most deserving. Those who deserved victory were those who displayed the martial virtues of courage and order. When the technology of weapons was usually equal, this was not an illogical stance to take.

The rune tyr was the promise of such a victory. But it can also be seen as the priest/king's dispensing of justice. The priest/king must see clearly what is right and where something has gone wrong, which leads to the next rune.

Moral value in peace and war is perhaps ensured by the rune boerc. Boerc stands for atonement.

Where victory in war is considered a moral victory it becomes imperative that the members of the army not have pollution in their souls. This was as true of the Germanic pagans as Cromwell's New Model Army—and in both cases seems to have been a concern only until it was time to sack the town. The duty of the priests was to ensure that atonement.

In times of peace, the priests or rulers had a similar duty of atonement politically and personally. It was assumed that there was, on a social and personal level, a natural state of health and smooth functioning. When something went wrong it was because of an imbalance or a pollution. In any of these cases an atonement was necessary to restore health.

The third rune of the aett is ehwis, which represents the twin gods, the Aclis. Only three runes specifically refer to a deity. Os in the first aettir is any god, though it is sometimes taken as Odin specifically. In the third aett are tyr and ehwis: cosmic justice and the gods who help people, respectively.

The Aclis seem to have been very close to the human race, even if they did not have a large formal cult. Their tendency to be the originators of various royal houses shows this. In an aett of the priest/king we would have to have some reference to the functions of the office and the gods as overseers of this. The notion of the divine king given special powers would last until the time of Charles I.

The atonement necessary was often a punishment. Sentencing was not to reform someone, but to provide atonement, which itself was thought to provide the basis for rehabilitation.

Ehwis is the rune of calling on divine aid, but also of strengthening the bonds of society. The atonement that was required made certain everyone reaffirmed the social norms.

The next rune is manu, which is the human being. It represents the race or the individual. So from cosmic justice or victory in war we devolve to atonement, the Aclis, and the race or the individual. Throughout we move from the most distant to the closest to us. The simple dichotomies of Freyja are not seen here. Here are functions of priesthood and rule, though more the former than the latter. The next four runes change this relationship.

Lagu as the sea, ing as the people, and odel as the property is almost a thumbnail sketch of Germanic society. Furthermore, if we start with manu we have the individual who is splashed with water at birth (lagu), becomes one of the people (ing), and inherrits property (odel).

In these last runes, though the priestly function is still described, rulership comes to the fore. The result is the last rune, doerg. This is light, shining day, salvation; the culmination of right rulership, right life, and the final event of initiation.

• ᚣ •

It is possible that a random collection of symbols, if they are strong enough, will always seem to have various interconnections. But the structure of the three aettir belies such a notion.

For a start, each of the three ends with a rune of positive nature and successively greater scope: wynn (glory), sighel (sun), and doerg (day). It implies the end of a course of instruction in

ᛗᛚᛏᚷᛘᚠᚾᛒᚦᚱᚲᚷᛈᚺᛏᛁᚷ ᛋᚲᚤᛋᛏᛒᛗᛚᛏᚷᛘᚠᚾᛒᚦᚱᚲᚷᛈᚺᛏᛁᚷᛋ

which the student has passed the tests and is ready to go on to the next step.

Each aett has certain runes which directly or indirectly cover similar concepts. Each, for example, has a rune for light. In Freyja this is ken, the torch. In Heimdall it is sighel, the sun; in Tir it is doerg, the radiant day. Note that the light is successively greater in power or covers a wider area.

Each aett has a rune referring to wealth or personal achievement. Freyja has feoh, Heimdall nyd, and Tir odel. All have a reference to the deities in os, sighel, and tyr and ehwis.

Each aett has a specific emphasis. Freyja has four runes of danger, evil, or cost to the runecaster (ur, thorn, rad, and gyfu); Heimdall has three (hoel, isa, and poerdh); Tir has, at most, one (lagu was sometimes the dangerous sea).

If we examine where similarities exist in two out of three aettir there is a much wider development. For example, only rad and poerdh deal with death; the aett of Tir has no such rune, as if priest/kings or the members of the third degree had faced and conquered the problem.

In the same way, the aett of Tir has no reference to ice or snow. Freyja has thorn and Heimdall has both hoel and isa. Yet it is Freyja's aett which lacks any reference to a weapon. Isa in Heimdall's aett and tyr in Tir's aett both refer to a spear. We should note that of the deities only Freyja was associated with peace rather than war.

When we look at functions rather than images there is even more overlap. Each aettir has at least one rune of protection, each has at least one rune useful as a good luck charm, each has a rune useful in healing magic, and so on.

It seems clear that there was an intended structure in these aettir; the runes were probably taught in three groups. But more than that, they were taught as a degreed system. Evidence for this is in the declining number of "negative" or "testing" runes, and the change from simple dichotomies to a more complex and panoramic use of the runes in the aettir.

This last point, incidentally, parallels the Tarot, where the Major Arcana begins with dichotomies or choices and winds up with groupings of cards showing different aspects of one principle. So in the beginning the choice is between guilessness and guile (Fool and Magician), the spiritual and chaste or the sensual and sensuous (High Priestess or Empress), and political or religious authority (Emperor or Hierophant). Later, there are groups of cards like Star, Moon, and Sun, or Justice, Hermit, and Wheel.

But more importantly for us, the aett of a rune has some effect on its magic. Ken is not the same as sighel or doerg, and there is more to the difference than mere scope or scale.

AETT MAGIC

The runes you choose to use, whether individually or combined, are affected by the aett in which they belong. There is more to a choice between ken, sighel, and doerg than scale or personal preference. There is a greater difference between isa and tyr, both involving a spear, than isa and hoel, both involving ice or winter.

This difference or similarity becomes extremely important in runic magic: a gift demands a gift; better not to pledge than to pledge overmuch. As I've said before, the runes are an ecological magic. It requires from you a necessary balance of intents, actions, and results. You need to make a statement or sacrifice before any significant magical work.

The nature of this balance differs depending on which aett is involved. This difference reflects the group of the society to which the rune belongs.

So feoh is wealth within Freyja's aett of the nurturer, while odel is wealth (or property) within the terms of the priest/king. These terms are as follows:

Freyja's aett of the nurturer is concerned with love, happiness, life, and enjoyment.

Heimdall's aett of the warrior deals with matters of achievement, money, victory, power, and success.

Tir's aett of the priest/king is used for matters of justice, spiritual achievement, understanding, establishing order, atonement, and all matters dealing with politics or rulership/authority.

ᛗᚪᛚᛉᛗᚠᚾᛈᚨᚱᚲᛇᛈᚺᛉᛁᛞᛋᛉᛦᛋᛏᛒᛗᛗᚪᛉᛗᚠᚾᛈᚨᚱᚲᛇᛈᚺᛉᛁᛞᛋ

When choosing a rune, then, one must look not only to its use or image, but to the aett in which it belongs. When combining runes, the same rules can apply.

For example, feoh is wealth in relation to personal happiness, livelihood, and enjoyment. It is not suitable when used in magic for becoming a millionaire because it doesn't take that much money to be happy on a personal scale.

On the other hand, odel is wealth which also indicates one's rank in society. Becoming a millionaire is quite germane to its function, if only because of the change in status involved.

Neither deals with money on its own terms: it is money to get happiness or money to establish a particular role in society. But it is Heimdall's own aett which involves money, even though it doesn't have a rune specifically for wealth.

This is because money, in the terms of Heimdall's aett, is a part of victory. It is built from associations of nyd, ger, and other runes. So nyd's general use of success includes monetary success, ger's comfort implies financial comfort, and so on.

But the aett of the rune has its own effect. Feoh could not be used to get enough money to dump a spouse; odel cannot be used to ensure success for the unjust. Moreover, to use feoh one could not sacrifice personal happiness to balance the money. What can you offer, then?

There are essentially two kinds of sacrifices suitable in runic magic: the gift to the gods and the personal sacrifice.

The gift refers to a physical object presented to the gods. This can be left in a sacred place (the common Greek and Roman custom), burned (akin to Chinese funeral practices), or buried. In all cases the object is meant as much as a votive offering as anything else: it is a declaration of your intent rather than a quid pro quo. As a general rule, the following are good examples of dedications for runic magic for significant goals.

Gifts related to Freyja's aett can include planting trees, choosing a bad patch of soil and rehabilitating it, cutting flowers and placing them on an altar, or making provisions for the poor (especially food for feoh or ur). Small gifts such as statuary can be stored in a sacred place, buried, or burned.

Gifts for Heimdall's aett can include weapons, coins, acts of courage, overcoming a fear or a bad habit, or acts of reconciliation.

Tir's aett can include almost any item of the previous two aettir. Significantly, it can also include other magical acts, such as undergoing a special initiatory journey through the astral realms, or using a ritual to enhance the justice of the world.

All three can include votive acts, such as lighting a candle and saying a mantra or a prayer for the length of the burning of the candle. They can include specific numbers or times of prayers to a particular deity associated with the rune or runes you wish to use.

In personal sacrifice, however, there is a different rule. Whereas with objects or actions you need items that match the character of the aett, personal sacrifice requires the opposite. Do not sacrifice love to please Freyja.

In other words, the sacrifice to be made must strengthen the precepts of the aett. In the case of physical objects this is done by similarity; in the case of personal lifestyle it is done by removing encumbrances.

So take the example of Freyja's aett: a personal sacrifice might be to spend more time with your children, bringing greater strength to that area of life. In return, the magic may eliminate financial or personal difficulties elsewhere in your life. It can mean a change of personality to become a more circumspect, caring person.

In cases of Heimdall's aett, personal sacrifice can include doing exercises to improve physical condition (both sports and exercise originated as preparations for war). Alternatives include shedding superfluities of life: cleaning out all your old junk is a simple example.

Runes of Tir's aett can be supported through acts of meditation or by becoming a calmer person. Matters of understanding and piety also form a foundation for personal sacrifice.

EXAMPLES

Say you want more money. First, check the runes which deal most closely with this. There are several runes which will work. There are feoh and ur in Freyja's aett; nyd, ger, and sighel in Heimdall's; and in Tir's aett, odel.

But what is the money for? Somebody out of work may only be looking for comfort—e.g., knowing he or she will be able to pay the rent next month. For this person, nyd is clearly inappropriate. Ur, with its implication of danger, is unlikely as well. This leaves odel and feoh.

Either one would be suitable. But feoh more closely approximates comfort. Odel would be more appropriate for the money to do something—e.g., the money for college fees. Assuming we settle on feoh, there are several gifts that might be made.

First, we can establish what we want the money for. We can restrict ourselves in that the money will be used for comforts and necessities rather than luxuries. If after receipt of the money there is a sudden purchase of foreign trips and gold bullion, expect severe reversals of fortune.

Individual gifts can be made, such as planting trees. The number of trees can be set numerologically, or can be one tree per every hundred or thousand dollars necessary. Or you can change your personality to strengthen the principles of Freyja—resolving not to think depressing thoughts for a period of three months, for example.

Let's take another example: suppose you want power. You've been at the bottom of the stack all your life and you want your card played. You want the chance to call your own shots in life, and don't care much whether the power is financial, political, or even simply a nebulous belief in power. We don't have to start with anything more than that rather vague statement to work out the appropriate rune(s) and gifts. And in this case there are many from which to choose.

If we're talking about a problem of not getting your share, we should look to Tir's aett. We're dealing with a question of justice and setting things right. The rune for that is tyr.

However, if you believe a previous life, pollution, or karmic debt is at the root of your troubles, boerc is the appropriate rune.

It may not be your pollution, but society's. The deck may be stacked against you. In such a case you may wish to call upon divine aid, so runes such as os or ehwis would be appropriate.

If you want money or property in proportions that make people respect you, use odel. If, however, it is the position of respect that is most important, you would be looking at the runes ing or isa.

And there are more general positive runes like ken, sighel, or doerg. And runes to attack enemies who hold you back (tyr), to protect you from them (eohl), to gain preferment from those higher up (lagu and doerg), or even to achieve success through a lifetime of right action (ger and eoh).

As you can see, there are many possibilities here. In this example we would need to narrow down exactly what is wanted and in what order. That is, take the matter in steps and use the magic item by item to achieve what you want.

If the odds are stacked against you, start with eohl. This is a rune of protection in Heimdall's aett. It can be used by drawing on its strength over time through ritual use, meditations, and the like.

The sacrifice to be made can be twofold. First, a change in lifestyle. Simply look for points of weakness and vow to slowly shut them down. If money is a problem, prepare to cut down on expenses and save. If you tend to get people angry, vow to cut out that habit.

The material sacrifice can be something appropriate to Heimdall's aett or the associated gods Magni and Modi. A small knife or a spearhead can be engraved with the rune eohl, or eohl on one side and tyr on the other. This can be buried or stored in a sacred place. Using it as a regular knife, however, is not a good idea. Some coins might be gifted. Wooden letter-openers can be carved or bought and burned.

Once protection is established, you need to look at the next step. This can be any one of several things, but we'll establish the aid of the gods. This means the rune ehwis.

This is in Tir's aett, so the sacrifice here could easily be a series of projections into the rune. Time spent watching a candle flame while silently carving and coloring the rune over and over could be another act of sacrifice. Time spent in self-improvement, to be worthy of the help of the twin gods, can be an important form of sacrifice.

With the aid of the Aclis through the rune ehwis, you would need to choose a third rune. The choice could be nyd to achieve the goal, or tyr to strengthen oneself. It is possible that the magic of the first two runes will choose the third for you. This may come by some coincidence, through inspiration, or in a dream. But the process should be clear.

At each stage another rune is chosen to overcome the problems at hand so that you can go a step further with your program. But when choosing multiple runes, particularly when they are to be used at the same time, the aettir have one more role to play.

RELATIONS BETWEEN AETTIR

It is common to combine runes to achieve a particular magical effect. Combining runes into a monogram was a common practice, one that continues today.

Suppose you want to combine the powers of nyd and ken, for example. These runes deal with harnessing and unleashing power; certainly an advantageous combination for, say, an athlete. But ken is in Freyja's aett and nyd is in Heimdall's. Does this cause problems?

Not really, but their combined strength may only be more precise and not actually twice as powerful than either rune separately. This is a case where two plus two, because of inefficiencies, may only make three, if even that much.

To maintain strength you must be aware of the aettir and the type of sacrifice involved in each. In this case Freyja is for the love of the sport, and nyd is for success and victory. The runes must be combined in such a way that ken makes you do your best, and nyd makes your best good enough to win.

ᚠᚢᚦᚨᚱᚲᚷᚹᚺᚾᛁᛃ᛫ᛇᛈᛉᛋᛏᛒᛖᛗᛚᛝᛞᚠᚢᚦᚨᚱᚲᚷᚹᚺᚾᛁᛃ᛫ᛇᛈᛉᛋᛏᛒ

It doesn't take two sacrifices for these runes. Better to have one overlapped sacrifice in the form of concentration on the combined pair. You must invest energy to achieve the desired results.

Only then, to seal the power, do you make a physical sacrifice. This can be as small as burning a candle or drinking an oath to the action.

We'll be examining this in more detail in the chapter on combining runes. But there are some rules we should remember when dealing with the aettir and choosing runes from them.

First, the functions of the runes in the aettir parallel each other, but those in successive aettir are more powerful and more general in purpose. So the success of nyd is more general than that of feoh. Where Freyja's aett has thorn the ice demon, Heimdall's has ice and winter, and Tir's simply has atonement.

Second, when combining runes do not simply pile up the runes of a whole aett or combine runes of the same function from each of the aettir. Some of the runes in the same aett counter each other, and parallel runes in different aettir do not always reinforce each other. So though os and ehwis can combine well, feoh and odel generally do not.

Third, do not combine dark runes or runes of danger. Thorn and hoel mix about as well as alcohol and gunpowder. There are some unavoidable exceptions in which the more difficult runes are mixed, but until you have experience, avoid them.

Fourth, when combining runes establish a key rune which will determine the "home" aett.

That being said, we will turn our attention back to the individual runes. We will need to learn them through meditation in order to draw from them the maximum magical value.

ᛗᛗᚠ ᚷᛞᚠᚾᛈᚦᚱ ᚲᚷᛈᚺᚤᛁ ᚦ ᛋᛣᚤ ᛋᛏᛒᛗᛗᚠ ᚷᛞᚠᚾᛈᚦᚱ ᚲᚷᛈᚺᚤᛁ ᚦ ᛋ

CHAPTER THREE

MEDITATION

How powerful are the runes? How much magic can you really do with them? These are two different questions, though most people don't recognize that fact.

Here's an analogy: if you have a power generator you can have thousands of megawatts of electricity. But the wire you use to conduct the electricity can't handle all of it at once. If too much electricity goes through a conductor, the conductor heats up and burns.

A common example is when a light bulb blows. It's a simple law of physics that one copper wire can't carry as much electricity as many, and a thin one can't carry as much as a thick one.

In the same way there is a great deal of energy in the runes, but it doesn't mean that the magic you can do is unlimited. You are a conductor of magical energy. When you begin you are like a single thin wire and can conduct only a small amount of energy. As you progress, you add more wires able to transmit increasing amounts of energy.

There are several ways to provide for this increase. In this chapter we examine one of these methods: meditation. In the next we will examine other exercises and techniques for summoning the power of the runes.

WHY MEDITATION?

The value of meditation lies in its ability to help you develop the set of complex associations necessary to call on all aspects of yourself in summoning the power of the runes.

The common conception is that the conscious mind is the center of our existence—that we are effectively unified beings. This has not always been the case: the *Illiad* and the *Odyssey* accept the idea that the individual psyche is a series of competing interests.

Magic has long accepted this notion. Different parts of our souls each have their own characteristics and their own interests. The task of the conscious mind is to get all of them to work in concert.

This is one reason why occultists of all types spend so much time working on correspondences. In the system of correspondences a planet is associated with a color, a number, a mantra or sound, a magical tool, and so on.

Thus we get the common descriptions that Mars is associated with red, with masculinity, with the day Tuesday (Tiew, another name for Tir or Tiwaz, was the god who gave his name to Tuesday), with the five-pointed star, etc. At the same time Venus is associated with green, with femininity, and so on.

By this system all principles have their own unique set of correspondences. By thinking of one, the others are called to mind. So the color red affects one part of us; the five-pointed star, another. As each part of the self is brought to bear with another layer of correspondences, more and more of the soul's energies are directed toward a particular result. Once a certain level is reached, a kind of connection is made and magic occurs.

In the runes there is such a set of correspondences. We began studying them in Chapter 1 when we went through the images, associated gods, magical uses, and individual strokes. What we need to do now is see how those associations can be strengthened in your mind so that you can build a greater level of energy and a stronger focus on your magical purposes.

ᛗᛖᛚᚱᛉᛗᚠᚾᚦᚨᚱᚲᚷᛉᛈᚺᛏᛁᛇᛋᚲᛉᚤᛋᛏᛒᛗᛗᛚᚱᛉᛗᚠᚾᚦᚨᚱᚲᚷᛉᛈᚺᛏᛁᛇᛋ

MEDITATION ON THE IMAGE

Images are far more powerful than words in many ways. According-ing to recent scientific experiments on monkeys, visualized images existed before mundane language, and even before the human race.

To gain familiarity with the runes you need to be familiar with their images. Pick a rune and look at it; become familiar with the shape of the rune.

Over time, begin to shift your attention to the image of the rune. For example, if you have chosen ger, its image is the harvest. So imagine a field of grain, ripe in the autumn sun.

Imagine it being harvested, the wheat being cut in swaths by sickles. The cut stalks are taken in bundles and beaten against stones to separate the grains. The bare stalks are then tied in bundles as fodder for the winter.

The grains themselves are taken and put in a tray. They are tossed into the air, the heavy wheat grains falling back to the tray and the light chaff being blown in the wind. The grain is then stored in sealed clay pots or silos.

When this work is done a festival is held. All the commu-nity has worked together on this one project. The high and the low, the rich and the poor, the judge and the thief have worked side by side.

In this meditation on the image of the rune, try to get behind the obvious. Do not simply conjure a static image; this does not involve the elements of your soul. You need to feel involvement—you need movement and as many associations and connections as possible.

So for feoh do not merely think of some static image of a cow or a slab of meat on a table. Instead think of the living ox, garlanded and feted. Think of the festival at which its meat will be served. Think of the poor waiting for the meat which they so rarely have. Think of those who have provided the beast, and gained religious and social merit for having done so.

See how different people see that ox as it is led, yoked, and prepared for slaughter. They see it as wealth and status, but also as something divine. It is a reflection of the creature central to the origin of the universe and the culture in which they live.

Whenever you examine the image of a rune you must invest this kind of energy in exploring its ramifications. The better you understand all the aspects of that rune's symbolism, the better you will be able to call on its energies.

COLOR AND NUMBER

The runes, though, are not only images, they also have numeric and color correspondences. These should be memorized and correlated. Which are the three black runes? Rad, isa, and ing—the journey to the otherworld, the spear, and the people. But their numbers are five, three, and six, respectively.

To understand the runes further, see how the color and number interrelate with the associations of the rune.

Take manu: one person or all. The number is four and the color is purple. Four is a number of stability, orderliness, and the material. The enemies of order in Germanic mythology were the frost giants.

We notice, then, that in all the myths no human is ever the ally of a frost giant. People become evil before Ragnarok, but their attacks are against each other. Many become the allies of the gods, standing with them at the end of days. This is a new insight to the Germanic myths, a deepening of the symbolism of the rune.

Four is also a material number, so we have the outer person represented here. This is not a description of the deepest part of us, but of our state of being.

The color of manu is purple, a color of passion and lust, but also power and royalty. This says manu describes humanity as orderly but subject to lusts—rather a good description.

When the lusts rule the person, he or she becomes the kind of crazed being mentioned in the opening words of the Ragnarok. This is an ice age, an axe age, a sword age in which men would sleep with their mothers and kill their brothers.

Each rune has such associations. We can extend this by examining runes of the same color and number and seeing where the runes are the same or different.

The other purple runes are os (the gods) and eohl (protection). The protection against our lusts are the gods. The religious impulse subsumes the lusts and keeps people—individuals or the race as a whole—on an even keel. Any quick check of history will not let you disagree too loudly over that.

The other runes with a value of four are os again and ger, the year or harvest. The establishment of order depends on the gods and the regularity of the harvest and the attendant festivals, chances to work together, and the availability of food during the hard winter.

Let us not forget that the coming of Ragnarok was signalled by the death of Balder and the consequent weakening of the gods. It was also heralded by three winters without intervening summers. Surely in this period food stores would be eliminated.

There would be no harvest. There would be fights for food. There would not be the regular common task or the festival to draw people together. The terrible age then begins to make more sense, and is described in some detail in the descriptions and associations of the runes.

Take any rune and examine its color and number. Find the other runes of the same color and number and see what they say about the original rune. Use the following correspondences for the numbers:

1: Unity, pioneering, sometimes brash and egocentric

2: Receptive, graceful, sometimes passive, absorbing and transforming

3: Expressive, lucky, expansive, friendly, jovial

4: Orderly, set, routine, material

5: Mercurial, human, collective

6: Gracious, home-loving, harmonious

7: Mystic, ideas ruling all else, in touch with the universe

8: Great success or failure, crash through or crash, great power

ᚠᚢᚦᚱᚲᚷᛈᚺᚾᛁᚴᛄᚲᚤᛋᛏᛒᛗᛁᛚᛉᛞᚠᚢᚦᚱᚲᚷᚺᚾᛁᚴᛄᚲᚤᛋᛏᛒ

For colors, the associations are:

Red: The physical, strength of will, the joyful

Brown: Ego, personal gain, how an individual affects things

Yellow: Intelligence, mysticism, communication, thought

Green: Creativity, sometimes cloying

Blue: Emotions, magic, images, power, expansive

Purple: Lusts, desires, royalty, authority

These are only brief descriptions. For more on color symbolism try S. G. J. Ousley's *Color Meditations*. For numerological symbolism try this author's *Understanding Numerology*.

We'll take another example and look at the rune's own associations. Let's take a less obvious example: nyd. Nyd is the power to achieve. Its color is blue; its number, two.

The number two is receptive, sometimes passive. But it is also absorbing and transforming, which is to say that to achieve the seemingly impossible, we must absorb and transform influences on us.

The greatest thing that keeps us from achievement is the belief that we are determined by the influences around us. If we're born poor we die poor, and the exceptions are just lucky. If you believe that, you won't achieve anything.

Success tends to come not to people who create something out of nothing, but to those who can absorb the events and influences around them and transform them so everything eventually works to their advantage.

The color blue is expansive. It is magic and images and power. To succeed we must have the power to bring our images (our ideas and plans) into existence. We must use the influences we have transmuted to shape the world until it conforms to the image we have for it.

Using these associations helps build an understanding of the individual runes. Quite often these associations do not simply expand or deepen an understanding, but reverse it. There are few people who would think of receptivity as part of an essential dynamic achieving the seemingly impossible. We are used to the concept of an active individual, one who reacts to a crisis and takes control. But we have become so enamored of "take control" that we forget about "react."

It will help in this exercise if you choose any rune and start with that. Write it down. To its left and right put the runes with the same number. Above and below put the runes of the same color. This gives you a visual image as a starting point when working on the associations.

Below, I've used ger as an example. To its left is os, to its right is manu. Above it is feoh, below it is odel.

The reader may think this is a lot of work for runic magic; that exploring the runes in this way will take so much time that the reader will never get to use them practically.

I should point out that these exercises are not what you have to do before any use. These exercises enhance your runic understanding and hence the magic.

It is true that it takes an enormous amount of time to work through all the runes. But one of the strengths of the system is that the runes themselves are a bottomless pit of wisdom, a mine that can never be exhausted: if they weren't, they wouldn't have sustained themselves over so long a time.

It is necessary to specialize in the practical use of some runes rather than others if these exercises are integral to their use. It seems likely that such specialization (apart from uses like divination) existed in the original period of the rune's use.

THE ASSOCIATED GOD

Each rune has an associated god, a deity who can be called upon to enhance that rune. The associated deity can also serve to deepen understanding of the rune in question.

When we say that the associated god of eoh is Forseti, the god of justice, we are making a significant esoteric statement. The rune is a symbol of restriction. It is a fir tree which symbolises immortality. This is a state to which humans cannot aspire, as the poisonous pine needles indicate.

The associated god is one of restriction as well. He punishes those who seek rewards to which they are not entitled. Justice means we refrain from doing things that are not right but are to our advantage. We accept that the poison bars us from immortality. Forseti as the god of justice oversees this.

Take another example: lagu is ruled by Aegir and Ran. The rune of the wave is ruled by the gods of the sea, which is most appropriate. But it goes further than this, in that lagu represents water in all its forms, just as do these two gods.

The rune is life-sustaining water, drinking beer, and death. Aegir and Ran give life and wealth; they are brewers whose cauldron is used to make beer for the gods and, in consequence, is something upon which oaths are taken. The sea is also the jaws of Aegir, and Ran drags people down in her net.

When considering the god of a rune, read the relevant myths and see the principles of the rune at work.

THE INDIVIDUAL STROKES

Of all the alphabets in the world, only the runes do not use curved lines in the formation of the letters. In all three of its variants this rule remains in force. There is no curved line among the some 240 different strokes in the three Futharks. This is clearly a rule far more important than ease of carving the runes into wood.

It was the first clue that the runes use the strokes to reinforce their magic, their meaning, and their syncretic unification of disparate magical practices and mythological beliefs of the Germanic pagans.

Over time the system became clearer, partly because some of the elements of the strokes are common to much of occultism up to and including complex Buddhist mandalas. It became clear that it was not only the stroke that was important, but to what position of the rune it was attached.

The top of the rune is the position of power; the bottom of the rune is the position of submission or response. No rune of any variant has a top or bottom bar. The rune lagu (ᛚ) has the same phonetic value as the Roman L, but this straight-lined letter was not adapted to the runes as was, for example, R.

And R itself might have been adapted with a top bar, making the top triangle a box or square or using a triangle with the base at the top. Instead it uses a diagonal so the letter rad (ᚱ) has only one point at the position of power.

A third example is ur (ᚢ), which has a diagonal bridging two verticals. A crossbar is not used—it never is. There is no rune with a horizontal stroke. This cannot be coincidence.

This means that the position of power or response is always emanating from a single source or series of single sources. Power is seen as emanating from discrete positions and having special, perhaps limited effects.

The vertical strokes generally relate to the formation of things. This can come in the form of the imposition of power or the approach to that power. It can be creative or destructive. But in all circumstances it will represent change and new creation.

Diagonals slope both up and down. These are devices of exchange. They represent solidification and the formation of stable conditions.

The center of a rune, where diagonals or diagonal and vertical often meet, is the place of becoming. Represented here is how a situation may be changed and altered through the various effects of power, response, and exchange.

When a stroke is carved from the position of power, it indicates power being imposed. The forces of destiny are at work;

ᚠᚢᚦᚨᚱᚲᚷᚹᚺᚾᛁᛃᛇᛈᛉᛊᛏᛒᛖᛗᛚᛜᛞᚠᚢᚦᚨᚱᚲᚷᚹᚺᚾᛁᛃᛇᛈᛉᛊᛏᛒ

often the situation is fluid and frequently out of the control of mundane forces.

A stroke carved toward the point of power indicates supplication or, sometimes, attack of divine forces—an attempt by the lower to take control of fundamental powers.

Where there are multiple points of power, as in the runes eohl (ᛉ) and gyfu (ᚷ), we are looking at a choice of power, the pagan notion that there is more than the epicenter involved.

Multiple points of supplication indicate rivals between which the points of power arbitrate. So in gyfu we have two points of power and two of supplication. The diagonals are the exchange or the structure.

It shows that the form itself, the structure of things, has come to dominate the whole of the matter. Gyfu does not make a profit, and the structure of things is bound together by the exchange.

In other words, gyfu is a rune about keeping things on an even keel. Its point of becoming is filled by the diagonals. The exchange goes on forever.

Take another case: ur (ᚢ). Here there is one point of power. From it comes a vertical representing the imposition of force directly to a position of supplication—the vertical line. It also has a diagonal, representing a structure being created prior to imposition or formation to a second point of supplication.

We have here formative power which acts directly as well as within a context, resulting in separate structures. In the same way Adumla formed the gods of Asgard and Vanaheim, but she also created the frost giants.

Moreover, ur shows power balancing between two supplications, an imposition which divides its strength. Because no line touches the point of becoming, there is no reconciliation. We would expect this to be corrected in some other rune, and a later version of ur has that very change with a third vertical between the other two. This third vertical reaches to the rune's center.

And take nyd (ᚾ): it is a single vertical and a diagonal meeting the vertical at the point of becoming. This is the imposition of formation which will forever yield a structure. It is a very

ᛗᛙᛚᚷᛞᚠᚢᛏᚦᚨᚱᚲᚹᛈᚺᚾᛁᛇᛋᚲᛦᛋᛏᛒᛗᛙᛚᚷᛞᚠᚢᛏᚦᚨᚱᚲᚹᛈᚺᛁᛇ

simple rune, but let's look at it more closely. We'll take its individual strokes and see how they fit with the description.

The vertical is carved down. In this the formative power is supreme. No opposition as yet exists; it is that adrenalin rush we feel when we have the momentum just right. We are certain we will win.

Then the diagonal is carved down through the vertical at the place of becoming. What we have then is an unfolding event, one that never quite becomes complete because of the balance between creative force and structure.

The diagonal is carved down, since it accepts the power of the formative force and seeks no more than to crystallize it into a stable structure.

In coloring, the diagonal is colored down. Its process of crystallization, the making of stable formative power, continues. In doing this it makes conditions ready for the vertical to be colored down. The formative power invests strength into the structure which has been created. The process, again, is permanent. This is a clue that the events nyd best affects are those which are determinate in our lives: that once having made the decision our lives are changed irrevocably.

So nyd is probably less useful for winning a poker game, more for getting a career change; less for winning a part in a play, more for getting noticed by reviewers; less for being inspired to write, more for getting a book published.

The same sort of analysis can be done for each of the runes. With this information is should be possible to create new runes. In fact, the extra runes in the Anglo-Saxon Futhark show that this did happen.

BRIDGING THE MEDITATIONS

From what we've said so far it would be possible to conclude that these meditations are discrete units. They contact different parts of our psyche and organize them to perform in concert. But the task is a bit more than that—we must also link the various meditations to get the best out of them.

ᚠᚢᚦᚨᚱᚲᚷᚹᚺᚾᛁᛇᛈᛉᛊᛏᛒᛖᛗᛚᛜᛞᚠᚢᚦᚨᚱᚲᚷᚹᚺᛁᛇᛈᛉᛊᛏᛒ

The image of a rune should be linked to its color, its number, its associated god, and its individual strokes. As you meditate on each, examine as well how the other categories reflect on the meditation you are performing.

For example, the strokes of nyd reflect its numeric value of two. The receptivity of two parallels the diagonal responding to the initial formative thrust of the vertical stroke.

It has a downward vertical thrust in both carving and coloring. This suggests the power of the color blue. That the rune comes to a balance, eternally affecting events, calls to mind blue's expansive qualities.

It is associated with the Norns: Urd, Verthandi, and Skuld. They are the Fates of the Germanic pagans who gave people not only their destinies but the means to that destiny. If they gave times of trouble to people, they also gave them the means to overcome those troubles. In the Germanic religion, it was not the end for which you were fated, but the situation. What you did in the situation proved your worthiness in life.

With nyd we have a reminder of your power to do the seemingly impossible. Use the powers of the depths of your soul and pass the test you were fated to take.

With such bridges between your meditations each rune can be understood from many viewpoints and in enormous detail. Doing this sets the foundation for the magical work you will do.

ONE COMPLETE EXAMPLE

We'll take one rune and follow through with the various meditations and bridges. The rune we'll choose is doerg (ᛞ), the last rune of the Futhark.

The image of doerg is a shining cart, the wheel of which is the sun disc. In this doerg is not the sun itself, but shining day. The influence of doerg begins when dawn is on the horizon but the sun is yet to rise. Conversely, its power continues after the sun has set.

We take this image, looking at the light as it begins on the horizon. It is banishing the darkness, just as the darkness in our

own souls can be banished by light. We could, with great benefit if some inconvenience, get up before the light and watch as
the eastern horizon grows lighter and lighter. Gloom replaces
darkness; light replaces gloom.

When the sun rises we should not see it as itself. We should
see it as a shining cart drawn by radiant steeds, with the sun as
its single wheel.

Little wonder that doerg's color is yellow. But eight, its
number, is a number of great success or great failure, of power,
and sometimes of excess. It is a number without compromise.

In the struggle between light and dark, too, there is no
compromise. The struggle is to avoid that terrible slide into the
days of Ragnarok, to put it off as long as possible.

Eight is also a number of great power, and doerg is a rune in
which the power of light exceeds our ability to control it. Yellow is the color of communication, thought, and mysticism. All
three are devices or recognitions of the banishment of darkness.

The salvation of doerg is mystical: the follower unified
with his or her deity. When we bring this back to the image of
the cart, we see ourselves on it. The cart is uncompromising,
demanding of us as much as we can give and more.

If we take the other runes of value eight and those which
are yellow, we get the figure below. In it ken is above, sighel
below; wynn to the left, sighel to the right:

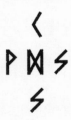

The runes ending the aettir are all positive. In the sense of
crash through or crash, of great success or great failure, they
clearly align with success, with crashing through. Wynn is
glory, meaning wisdom and ability; sighel is the sun, transcen-

ᚠᚢᚦᚨᚱᚲᚷᚹᚺᚾᛁᛃᛇᛈᛉᛊᛏᛒᛖᛗᛚᛜᚠᚢᚦᚨᚱᚲᚷᚹᚺᚾᛁᛃᛇᛈᛉᛊᛏ

dent power. Between the three there is strong reinforcement, just as there is between the three yellow runes.

These are ken, sighel, and doerg. Respectively, they are the harnessed power of light, the transcendent power of the sun, and the final banishment of the darkness.

In both cases we have an increasing scope of action and increasing power. Wisdom (wynn) leads us to transcendent power (sighel), which eventually becomes the means of the triumph of light (doerg). Similarly, harnessing the power (ken) leads us to the power of transcendence (sighel), which leads to the banishment of darkness within ourselves (doerg).

Thus the color and the number describe the internal and external view of the light-dark or order-chaos polarity. It is both the banishment of darkness in the form of external enemies and of the darkness within ourselves which lead us to perform actions that are not right.

When we consider the light of day banishing night we should regard it in the same way. The glow on the horizon represents wisdom. The sunrise represents sighel as transcendent power. The brightness of day peaks at high noon.

We should also think of the same process in our own soul. When we harness power, its use leads us back to its origin, the original power of transcendence. This in turn transforms our very selves.

In the same way, wisdom leads us to that transcendent power. Finding that source of wisdom will itself lead to the transcendent power of which the wisdom is an outer expression. It should also remind us that a wise person comes to the gods sooner than a foolish one does.

The associated god is Balder. He was the deity who was, through Loki's trickery, killed by Hoder. He was a deity of light, justice, and poetry; his death was the beginning of Ragnarok.

Beyond Ragnarok, even in the form in which we know it, there lay another world which was pure and new. Despite Balder's death, despite the defeat of the gods, the power of light could not be extinguished.

We should point out, of course, that Ragnarok was originally not the destruction of the world, but its purification. Odin might be swallowed by Fenrir, but the animal would meet its death by having its jaws spread wide—something which indicates Odin's rescue. However, the place for a restoration of the esoteric meaning of the Germanic myths is elsewhere.

We should note that so long as the gods have Balder with them, Ragnarok cannot be. So long as we as individuals have the light of doerg, we cannot be pulled down into the darkness. Balder the god and doerg the rune both represent the radiant power, the transcendent mysticism which is an impenetrable protection against wrong thought and dark action.

That the rune has a value of eight ties in well with the myth of Balder. While he is alive the gods are eternally safe from destruction. Success in some form is absolutely guaranteed. It assures them great power over the frost giants.

When Balder dies, the situation is no longer guaranteed. Quite the opposite—the loss of Balder guarantees the defeat of the gods. This is great success or great failure, just as the number eight requires.

This same principle applies to the individual strokes of the rune. These are two verticals and two diagonals which meet at the point of becoming. Thus power is necessary to maintain the exchange.

Remember, we said that the individual strokes of doerg were an indication of an established structure which continues indefinitely. In this case, the verticals indicate that the structure must be maintained or support some other structure in turn. In the case of the myth of Balder, it is both.

The first stroke is the left vertical down: fate gives its decree about Balder. Then the diagonal is carved up and to the right. The exchange begins; formative power is crystallized in a way that does not return to the source.

When Balder has his dreams predicting his death, no one goes to the Norns. They go to Hel and Niflheim.

Hel (a daughter of Loki, by the way) gives her decree that Balder shall come. The second source of power has made its

ᚠᚢᚦᚨᚱᚲᚷᚹᚺᚾᛁᛃᛇᛈᛉᛊᛏᛒᛗᛚᛜᛞᚠᚢᚦᚨᚱᚲᚷᚹᚺᚾᛁᛃᛊᛚᚲᛁᛊᛏᛒ

decree; the right vertical is carved down. Then the second diagonal is carved up and to the left. The oath is taken from all the objects in the world that they shall not harm Balder—bar mistletoe, which seems insignificant.

In this the structure is set to continue, for the Norns have not changed their statement. The supplication is lost in the balanced structure which is continuing, as shown by the meeting of diagonals at the point of becoming.

The coloring starts with the vertical stroke downward. This is the death of Balder. The command is then sent that if all nature weeps for Balder, he shall be returned to the gods.

These two commands operate in tandem, the death and the mourning, because they both are requirements. The world is then searched high and low and everything agrees to weep for Balder—presumably even the mistletoe that killed him.

This search is represented by coloring the diagonals down and to the right and up and to the right. There is conflict here, for one being, Thokk the giantess, refuses to weep. Though everything else flowed with the command she went against it and, in conflict with the others, set up the ever-becoming. The middle of the rune is the place of this conflict, setting up the next stage.

But the myth and the strokes tell us another thing about the image. We see the early dawn and the dew which is all nature weeping for Balder, weeping for the light to make it return.

But ice, Thokk, does not form dew. It is water that is dry just as Thokk says she will weep dry tears. It is not warmed by the dawn, nor can the dawn melt it. The final vertical is carved.

In this we can see how each form of meditation can enhance the others. It builds each rune into a vast web of understanding, which in turn makes it easier to use the magic of the rune. It is an exercise well rewarded.

ᛗᛗᛚᚪᛞᚠᚾᚦᚱᚳᚷᛈᚻᛏᛁᛂᛋᚳᛃᛇᛏᛒᛗᛗᛚᚪᛞᚠᚾᚦᚱᚳᚷᛈᚻᛏᛁᛂᛋ

NEW MYTHS

There is one more meditative tool I wish to bring up here: myth creation. The easiest way to explain this is with an example:

A **tame ox,** the child of a **wild ox,** was tormented by a **demon** who did not wish the animal to be duly sacrificed to the **gods.** So the demon travelled to the **otherworld** to search out a way to stop the **torchlight festival.** Such a **gift** might allow the gods to give more **wisdom** to humanity.

The words in boldface are the images of the runes of Freyja's aett of the Elder Futhark. The images become the pegs upon which a story is built.

This can be done with virtually any esoteric alphabet except the Enochian. This is because the Enochian alphabet does not have magical images for each letter.

In the Hebrew alphabet, for example, we could open a myth as follows:

Behind his **ox** in the fields, a man does not see when his **house** is visited by a merchant whose **camel** bears great riches. This beast of burden waits outside his **door** and looks plaintively in the **window,** hoping the owner of the house shall return.

In this the boldface words are aleph, beth, gimel, daleth, and he, the first five letters of the Hebrew alphabet.

This task is one you will need to do if you wish to plumb some of the deeper mysteries of any magical alphabet, not just the runes. There is a specific exercise with it.

You must not only write a myth for the whole Futhark, you need to choose runes at random. That is, a random order and a random number of runes. These runes, in the order in which you select them, must be the basis for a new myth.

In using the runes as the pegs of this myth you can use any part of their meaning, though the image is usually the easiest. But you can use the associated god or the magical uses as the basis of the myth. In this you may think the word "myth" overblown, and the word "fable" more appropriate. But the

ᚠᚢᚦᚨᚱᚲᚷᚹᚺᚾᛁᛃᛇᛈᛉᛋᛏᛒᛖᛗᛚᛜᛞᚠᚢᚦᚨᚱᚲᚷᚹᚺᚾᛁᛃᛇᛈᛉᛋᛏᛒ

story can also provide the basis of ritual action, which literally makes it a myth.

A myth (Greek *muthus*) was a story paired with a *dromenon* (ritual). These stories can be the basis of ritual plays or ritual actions.

At the simplest level, the use of ken at least implies something like a torch and using it in a ritual about the sight. Lagu would indicate drinking beer or being splashed with water. Feoh and ger might be eating meat and bread, respectively.

Thus what appears at first sight to be a random collection of letters becomes a doorway into both a magical ritual and a mythic representation of the truths those letters hold. We'll find this a valuable tool when combining runes into talismans and the like.

This is not a limitation in runic work. We should note that if we were to use the whole Futhark there would be something like 2,583,200,000,000,000,000,000 ritual-myths of the runes. This number increases when we include groups of less than the whole Futhark and when we remember that the same rune might represent a thing, an event, a god, or a ritual action.

To show the permutations, let's take the first aett again, and see how the same myth could have been written with slightly different associations:

Freyja had gone to **Adumla** to ensure the fertility of the world. But an **ice demon** heard her call the cow, and resolved that no god, not even **Odin,** could make the earth fruitful again. So he stole the feather form of Freyja to stop her **journey to the underworld.** The demon stole her **magic powers of light** to use for his own ends.

Freyja went to **Hoder,** asking his aid. But Hoder was unmoved.

"I am blind," he said, "and can be no more help than witness for you. Go, instead, to **Skirnir.** That bright and fast god did well enough for your brother Freyer. I am sure he will do well for you."

Freyja thought Hoder right, and thanked him before making her way to the fast and clever god.

ᛗᛒᛚᚪᛗᚠᚾᚦᚨᚱ᚜ᚷᛈᚻᛏᛁᚴ᛬ᛢᚴᚤᛏᛒᛗᛒᛚᚪᛗᚠᚾᚦᚨᚱ᚜ᚷᛈᚻᛏᛁᚴ᛬ᛢ

Here the boldface words represent exactly the same runes as the previous Futhark myth. It is an equally valid esoteric story. Similarly, one could consider the same aett as the basis of ritual.

Feoh gives us the idea of addressing the opening prayer of the ritual to Freyja, and to seek from it results appropriate to that goddess.

Ur suggests releasing a captured animal.

Thorn is the ice demon who opposes the kind of fruitfulness appropriate to the Vanir goddess.

Os can be any god, so we can again address Freyja. With the image of a pine tree we can ritually place pine branches and pine cones.

Rad is the otherworld. It is a symbol of change, so here Freyja can be asked for blessings or to bring about a particular change. As the journey, it might be the appropriate point to commence an astral projection or ritual divination. If so, someone else would have to carry out the next ritual steps for you.

Ken is the torch, so we have the lighting of torches (or more practically, candles) and carrying them in procession.

Gyfu reminds us to provide a "gift for a gift." A sacrifice is made in the form of an oath to change, or perhaps the laying of flowers or the lighting of incense.

Wynn as glory becomes the closing of the ritual with thanks for the blessing Freyja will undoubtedly provide. If the objective of the ritual is astral projection or divination, this is a point at which it could be done.

If you projected at rad, you would use wynn as the point of return, putting away your divinatory runes, and so on.

CONCLUSION

By these steps you can gain a broad range of knowledge about the runes. You can still use them without having done these exercises, but not as well. Even a natural athlete does better with training and practice.

Moreover, as you do the exercises you become better aware of the their length and breadth and the symbolic potency which lies behind the runes. Length and breadth, that is, but not depth. There is another set of exercises necessary to unleash the magical power of any system. Those are what we will turn to next.

With these exercises you will gain the cooperation of different parts of your soul. This alone will mark you as more advanced than most of the people in the world. But it is far from the end of the path. You have many wires instead of one; you must now get larger wires. Which is to say, having trained the elements of your soul to work together, you need to learn to strengthen those elements.

ᛗᛘᛚᛉᛞᚠᚾᚦᚨᚱᚲᚷᚹᚻᚤᛁᛝᛋᚲᛦᛏᛒᛗᛘᛚᛉᛞᚠᚾᚦᚨᚱᚲᚷᚹᚻᚤᛁᛝᛋ

CHAPTER FOUR

SUMMONING THE POWER OF THE RUNES

To summon the power of a rune does not require a magical temple: much of the Germanic pagan world was itinerant if not nomadic. Summoning power does not require magical tools such as the swords, cups, pentacles, wands, and daggers to which many books refer. A properly trained runecaster can, naked and alone, still successfully call upon the powers of the runes. There are variations to the method, but it basically goes like this.

The runecaster calms his or her mind, possibly with relaxation and deep breathing exercises. All mundane thoughts are dismissed.

Concentrating his or her entire attention on the task, the runecaster raises a hand. The runecaster draws the first stroke of the rune that has been chosen for the spell. As his or her hand moves, the runecaster sees blue-white light forming a trail behind it.

This light is imagined so strongly that the runecaster sees it as if it were drawn with a marker. In many cases the brain will react as if this astral light had physical reality. In a few remarkable cases it seems this light can be photographed—though to be fair, such examples could be easily faked or created by accident.

While the first stroke is made, the runecaster recites the line of that stroke as given in Chapter 1. At the same time the runecaster visualizes the magical image of the rune, keeping this image at a less direct positioning in his or her consciousness.

The strokes continue until the rune is "carved." The runecaster continues the task by coloring the rune. In this case each stroke trails the color of the rune. The runecaster must not only see the light, he or she must see it in the appropriate color, and it must fully take over the blue-white light that had gone before.

The runecaster then continues with the lines to be said in coloring the runes. Like the words for carving, these may be said internally or out loud.

The runecaster will also continue with whatever breathing exercise or rhythm, relaxation of muscles, or similar discipline his or her training requires or allows.

When the rune is colored and seems to stand before the runecaster with physical reality, concentration shifts. The image of the rune which has been continued through all the previous events now comes into play.

The rune is invested with greater energy; it is brought forward to take on the greater potency of concentration. The runecaster shifts the image so it conforms with what he or she wants the rune to do.

If he or she wishes to win love, the image confirms this. If he or she wants wisdom, the image permits this. In all cases, the shift must be consistent with the correspondences of the rune. The color, number, and all other correspondences must work with the rune and not against it.

The runecaster then recites a poem or statement confirming the coming reality of what he or she desires. This is the part of the spell that others are most likely to hear, so it is the part most often mentioned in esoteric lore.

During this whole rite the runecaster must use his or her magical skills to find, tap, conduct, concentrate, and release into the spell the magical energy required to make it work.

Magic can be hard work. We all use it a little bit—if you can't, you die. But this structure of spells can be a different kettle of fish altogether.

Fortunately, the finding and tapping of magical energy is already accomplished; this was learned in the last chapter. That was why you spent so much time doing all those seemingly interminable meditations. Each one took a different part of your soul and trained it to tap a little more magical energy. It helped your mind, body, and soul to coordinate their activities, and direct them all to a single end.

But that isn't the whole of the task. These different aspects all need to be involved in casting the spell. But in most people they are not of equal strength. Some are quite good; most are rather weak because we do not habitually use them.

To overcome this we need to exercise. It means slow work, and it is not the kind of magical exercise that appeals to the consciousness junkie. It isn't "a little bit of this and a little bit of that—and please make it entertaining."

It is better to do one exercise thoroughly than to do all perfunctorily. It is better to do an exercise for five minutes a day for a dozen days rather than do it once for an hour (or two, or four).

On the other hand, none of these exercises are difficult in themselves. They are merely a natural extension of what we do on a daily basis, just as jogging is a kind of hyped-up walking.

Nor is it necessary to master them all. As you practice each and gain skill in it, the benefits will flow automatically to your magic. A strong will, for example, will help compensate for poor visualization; good projection will overcome poor relaxation. With that in mind we will turn to the individual exercises.

RELAXATION

It is not so much because of the nature of magic that this exercise needs to be learned, rather it is the nature of the age of anxiety in which we live. Whatever the cause, the reality is that most of us live with our muscles subconsciously tensed, with worries lurking behind the field of our attention. Yet the exercise of muscle relaxation is easy to do.

EXERCISE 1

First, find a place where you won't be disturbed for a few minutes. Once you've mastered the exercise you'll be able to do it

ᚠᚢᚦᚨᚱᚲᚷᚹᚺᚾᛁᛇᛃᚲᛦᛈᛏᛒᛖᛗᛚᛜᚠᚢᚦᚨᚱᚲᚷᚹᚺᚾᛁᛇᛃᚲᛦᛈᛏᛒ

anywhere, but for now I'll be asking you to shift around in a manner that might draw attention.

All you need to do is concentrate on each muscle in turn, turning your attention to it and making it relax. Sometimes, if you find it difficult to relax a muscle, you should tighten it first, then relax it.

Where you begin this exercise is up to you. In this case, we'll start with your face.

Concentrate on your jaw muscles. Are your teeth clenched tightly? Does your forehead feel tight? It is surprising how often people clench their jaws or grind their teeth in the urge to suppress anxiety.

Slacken the muscles of your jaw. You don't have to let your mouth drop open, just let the muscles loosen. Arch your eyebrows and let them drop; let the muscles in your forehead relax. Close your eyes, then behind the lids look left, then right, then up, then down.

Relax the muscles in your neck. Note that if you don't, if you stop right now, the tension in your neck will force the muscles in your face to tighten again.

Shift your head from side to side. Nod your head down, to the right, back, and to the left.

Now let your arms relax. It may help if you raise them and tense the muscles a bit. Stretch them. Then let them fall back down to hang limply at your sides.

Now relax your chest and stomach muscles.

Turn to your legs. As you did with your arms, raise them, tense them, stretch them out, and let them drop.

As a last effort, will your toes and feet to relax.

As you practice this exercise you will feel the need for physical movement diminish. Eventually you need only stop for a second and let the feeling of relaxation wash over you.

You can reinforce this and make access to the exercise easier. Just say to yourself something like "I will now relax" before doing your exercise. Eventually your body will react to the words like Pavlov's dogs salivating at the sound of a bell. You will say the phrase and a feeling of relaxation will wash over you.

ᛗᛗᚠᛉᛗᚠᚢᛈᚦᚱᚲᚷᛈᚺᛁᛉᛋᚲᚤᛋᛏᛒᛗᛗᚠᛉᛗᚠᚢᛈᚦᚱᚲᚷᛈᚺᛁᛉᛋ

VISUALIZATION

Visualization is essential to working with the runes. Good visualization will cover many other weaknesses more easily than another strength will cover for weakness of visualization.

For some people this comes easily, for others it can seem exceedingly difficult. Again, it is partly a matter of culture. Though we are said to live in a highly visual age, the various images of television, special effects, and the like are dished up to us like so much candy. This affects our ability to visualize like a steady diet of candy affects our athletic prowess.

In earlier eras people had to visualize more, and so it came more easily to them. They had to enhance the imagery of the stage, they had to visualize the words of novels, and in many cases they learned to do things through visualization rather than verbal recitation.

That is, when doing things like harvesting crops, the constant sweep of the scythe was done not through internal verbalization (swing, return, aim, swing) but through visualizing the task and letting the body fulfill what the mind envisioned.

Even without these advantages we can still benefit from visualization. Start by closing your eyes and rolling them up under the lids. If you find this easy to do, visualization should offer you relatively little trouble. If you can't or find it very discomforting, you will need a trick that will boost your abilities. Fortunately the boost doesn't mean more exercise, just a change to the one you're about to read.

EXERCISE 2

For this visualization exercise you will need a blank space such as a smooth wall or a large piece of paper. In both cases the field should be white or a light gray, if possible, but some color is acceptable.

Stand before the field and relax. Then raise one hand and trace a simple geometric figure. This can be a line, a square, a triangle, a circle, anything. As you move your hand you should see a thin line of blue-white light forming the figure as you trace it.

ᚠᚢᚦᚨᚱᚲᚷᚹᚺᚾᛁᛇ�ᛋᛏᛒᛗᛗᛚᛦᛞᚠᚢᚦᚨᚱᚲᚷᚹᚺᚾᛁᛇᛋᛏᛒ

The line will be very faint at first, if you can see it at all. Many people find that it takes some time to see the line, and it is safest to assume you are one of these people. Give yourself three weeks of work before you will truly begin to see the line you draw.

When you first see the light it is only in what can be described as being seen at the back of the skull. It is more a case of knowing what should be there than it actually existing.

With time you will begin to see the line more and more clearly. Eventually the visualization simply "moves forward" in your skull. You see the line your hand has drawn clearly, seemingly objectively. The line now obscures what lies behind it.

This is the first big step in visualization. Once you've taken it, practice becomes far more interesting.

In all these cases, you need to dismiss the image after you've made a tracing. For most, a simple wave of the arm suffices. This action erases the lines. Others need to dismiss the line more formally, saying "I banish this form, for it has served my purpose," or some similar statement. This is a matter of personal preference.

The next step is to gain more control over the line. To do this, you have to stop using your hands.

EXERCISE 3

Working at your usual place, stand and concentrate. Form your magical energies into a small pinpoint of blue-white light. With your will alone, move that light to trace a line, and then to draw the figure you wish it to draw.

It sounds the same as before, but this is more difficult. The pinpoint of light will try to dance, to get away, to spoil the drawing by making what can only be considered to be a caricature of the thing. Your square becomes a kite; your circle, a kind of pear.

There is no easy cure for this. You simply have to wrestle it under control so often that whatever inside you is resisting simply gives up. It suddenly becomes easy to control the pinpoint of light and to make it draw any shape you want.

ᛗᚾᛚ ᚷᛗᚠᚾᛓᚨᚱ ᚲᚷᛈᚺᛏᛁᚴ ᛋᛚᚤᛋᛏᛒᛗᚾᛚ ᚷᛗᚠᚾᛓᚨᚱ ᚲᚷᛈᚺᛏᛁᚴ

There is a second element to visualization, however—color. There is an exercise to help this.

EXERCISE 4

All you need to do is relax, close your eyes, and think about a particular color. Try to get the color to flood your mind until you see it on the back of your eyes.

Again, it will start as an idea before it is a reality. But for those who find visualization difficult at the best of times, there is a trick to help. We can use spoken words to help us visualize.

For the visualization of color you need only tell yourself that you will see that color. For example, "I am going to see red. It will flood my field of vision; I will see red clearly and completely." Though it doesn't work instantly, it does tend to reduce the time before successful visualization.

The same trick can work for tracing the line. Before your exercise you can say, "I will now trace a square, and as my hand moves I will see the light of magic forming the square."

Even when you've learned that exercise you can use your words to help in the next one. This time just say, "I will now be tracing by the power of my will. The light will be under my control at all times." The final form of the words, of course, will be up to you.

In this way your words, which you are used to controlling, can help establish control over visualization. But this is not the whole of the matter. The runes not only use visualization for the line but have a magical image to be used.

These images can be developed, too. Through practice you can build their strength and complexity. Practicing with them now helps with astral projection later on.

EXERCISE 5

Begin by choosing any of the images of the runes. It is a matter of preference, but I suggest you start with one of the more positive examples.

Visualize the magical image of this rune as best you can. This doesn't simply mean in detail, it means in depth. When most people first visualize these scenes, it's as if they were watching a movie (visualization predates the movies, and may help to explain the silver screen's great success). Make the image like a three-dimensional scene through which you walk.

One simple example is ken, a lit torch. You should in your imagination see the torch burning, but take care that the flames dance realistically. In your imagination, take a tour around the torch; see it from different angles.

If it's on a stick rather than milled wood it will look different from different angles. The wood may have a knot on one side.

After a while you will begin to fill in details of the background. Is the torch alone or are there several? Is it stationary or moving? Is someone holding it or is it put into the ground? As you ask these questions you will begin to see the details of the scene around the torch.

For a while these details may look pale and quite flat, even cartoonish. But as you continue, these extra details will become filled out as three-dimensional objects.

There are two things to note with this exercise. First, it is an aid to astral projection because it sensitizes you to the kind of awareness you need for that exercise. It is not astral projection itself, because these figures have only subjective reality.

Second, you can interpret the scenes much as you would interpret dreams. What you find in the imaginary scenes is a product of your unconscious, much as dreams are, and these scenes are subject to much the same laws. However, relatively more emphasis should be placed on what you find than what you do not.

Visualization is a great aid to runic magic, but there is a little more to the matter than this. You will also need to strengthen your will and concentration to develop your powers of runic magic.

WILL

There are several exercises to develop will; we'll start with the simplest of them. This trains the faculty of will we most associate with the term.

EXERCISE 6

All you need to do is pick a useless, boring task. The boring part is important because you're going to decide to do this task for a given number of minutes and carry it through.

For example, you might choose to stand on one foot for six minutes. As long as this doesn't cause physical problems (choosing to hold heavy weights for long periods is not a good idea), it's a good choice. Other tasks include standing on a chair, sitting (nearly) motionless while looking at a blank wall (not doing your visualization exercises), counting dots on a sheet of paper, and other meaningless tasks.

Set a period of time to do these things. Start with just a couple of minutes. Gradually extend the time until you do these tasks for up to six minutes.

One trick that helps, at least in the beginning, is to have someone with a watch tell you the time every fifteen seconds or so. The feedback of this helps you get to the goal.

For some exercises, though, you can't use a watch for yourself. If you stare at a wall, for example, looking at your watch breaks the concentration. In these cases you will need to set an alarm clock or stopwatch for the time you need. But unlike many occult exercises, the exact time spent on this one doesn't matter. The effort that you make will do much to build your willpower and bring you to readiness for the next step.

EXERCISE 7

You will need to fill your mind with a single thought—in this case, a particular shape. For this exercise you will need some white cardboard, some colored paper, and a marker or a felt-tip pen. The colored paper should not have much texture: use smooth rather than rough or woven paper.

Choose a shape with which you want to work. Cut out that shape from the colored paper. To do this properly you'll need a straightedge or compass and a pencil to measure out the figure. Put the glue on the side with the pencil marks so you won't see them.

You don't need a large image or card—something about the size of a playing or Tarot card is fine. In fact, the simpler versions of such cards often prove useful in this exercise.

Glue the colored shape onto the middle of the white cardboard. If you use a marker it isn't a cut-out shape you will use, but one of the runes. This has to be drawn very carefully, and the ink must not bleed or leave streaks in its trail. The lines it forms should be solid and thick. The color of the marker should match the color of the rune. If the rune is white you can use white ink on black or dark-gray paper, or use a light-gray marker.

Draw the rune on the cardboard, making certain that it is correctly proportioned and all the lines are straight. Again, use a straightedge to make sure of the strokes.

You don't have to carve and color according to the magical strokes, because this rune and cardboard will not be used in that manner. Instead, set the cardboard up so it stands a convenient distance from you. You should be able to see the whole of the shape or the rune without moving your eyes. This point is very important: if the edges of the shape seem fuzzy, your eyes will automatically move to take in the image. Once you do that you distract yourself.

Set the device far enough away so that you can see all of it without moving your eyes, yet close enough that the image is still distinct. It does no good to avoid moving your eyes if you have to squint. In fact, squinting is worse. If you have to make a choice, bring the image closer and live with the occasional twitch of the eye.

Once you have the card at a comfortable distance, dismiss all daily thoughts. A shrug of the shoulders or other physical actions can help you do this, as can your relaxation exercises.

Now, stare at the image on the card. Let your mind concentrate on it and only on it. Let nothing else enter your mind.

Of course, as is common with these things, other thoughts will intrude immediately. Itches and twitches will appear suddenly. The only recourse you have is to wrestle them down with your mind.

If necessary, words can also help with this exercise. Tell yourself, "I am going to concentrate on this [name of image]. I will consider it and nothing else."

Over time the intruding thoughts will diminish, and the itches will go away (without your scratching them). Then, all of a sudden, you will have nothing in your mind but the image in front of you.

If you're like most people, your immediate reaction is something along the lines of "I did it!" This, naturally, breaks your concentration. The important point is not how long you've done it, but that you've done it at all. With practice the periods of total concentration get longer. They don't have to be longer than about three minutes, for that is about as long as it takes to summon the power of even the most complex rune.

Having gained the power of concentration you can move on to extending it, fitting its abilities into those most needed for using the runes. To do this we have to turn back to the exercise of visualization.

EXERCISE 8

You will again have to work with the image of the rune, visualizing it in the three-dimensional detail you developed. This time, however, you need to do the visualization without distraction.

In other words, you're going to have to visualize the image of the rune without any other thoughts. This is hard to do for any length of time. For one thing, you will frequently find that you have been pursuing a different line of thought for a considerable period of time.

You should do your relaxation exercise before you start. Take a few deep breaths and verbally tell yourself what you plan to do. "I am now going to visualize the image of the rune [name]. I will think only of it and nothing else."

Then begin visualizing the rune's image. Make it three-dimensional, but understand that the image will probably be somewhat less intense than you are normally used to.

You may be lucky. By now some people find slipping into exercises very easy, and progress from stage to stage provides little difficulty. For others, each exercise requires a new effort. However, by the stage indicated by this exercise you will have already progressed some distance down the path of real magical work.

You will find the runes easier to call upon, and their powers more effective in your life. Spells begin to have more dramatic effects. For example, spells for good luck or success tend to be followed with distinct benefits like promotions or breakthroughs in life. Many would wish to stop here. But the stronger magics, the ones which change you or which most effectively benefit lives other than yours, still lie ahead.

When you can visualize the rune's image for five minutes without a single intervening thought, you're ready for the last exercise in will. Again, it builds on your experience with visualization exercises.

EXERCISE 9

You will need to trace the rune using your magic light. For the moment you do not have to recite the words of the carving or coloring, nor do you have to do the individual strokes in order. However, if you can do them in order it is best to do so. It can help with memorization of the strokes.

Stand in front of the large piece of paper against which you trace images. In this case you won't trace a simple geometric figure, but you'll trace the runes one by one.

Start your rune by tracing it out in blue-white light. Use your hand when you start because it makes control much easier. Later, if you wish, you can draw with just your will.

Draw the whole rune, then go over it again in the color of the rune. So to draw nyd (ᚾ), start by drawing it in blue-white,

ᛗᛗᛚᛣᛗᚠᚾᚦᚨᚱᚲᚷᛈᚻᛏᛁᛇᛃᛣᚣᛋᛒᛗᛗᛚᛣᛗᚠᚾᚦᚨᚱᚲᚷᛈᚻᛏᛁᛇᛃ

then draw it in true blue. This blue should be as rich as possible.

Similarly, if you draw manu (ᛘ), you draw it first in blue-white and then in a verdant purple. Ehwis (ᛗ) is drawn in blue-white and then in true and preferably brilliant white.

You should be able to go through the entire drawing of the rune without any intervening thoughts whatsoever. When you can do this for all 24 runes you're ready to go on to the next exercise, which in a sense is not an exercise at all, but a preparation.

PURIFICATION

The modern concept of pollution, when stripped of scientific jargon, is a revival of a pagan concept. The word originally was pagan, one of the few words of the pagan religion neither taken over nor degraded by Christianity. The word comes from Latin and means "to defile."

The counter state to pollution was purity, which originally meant unstained. Priests should wear unstained clothes, and their implements must be clean when they approach the gods. They must perform the rites properly, without error.

But over time purity became a matter of the soul. When the aura is seen, it sometimes shows what looks like stains or tears. This represents damage to the envelope and is sometimes connected with the unworthy thoughts of the person whose aura it is.

So over time the concept of pollution moved from ritual terminology to a spiritual or moral concept. This is a development which can be identified in several pagan mythologies.

An example of this is in the Greek myth of Theseus and Herakles. Herakles, driven mad by Hera, killed his wife. When Theseus clasped his cousin's hands he not only shared the physical stain of blood but the moral stain as well. He, too, had to purify himself.

In Persia, Zoroaster the prophet defined pollution, its causes, and its purification for the religion of the Mazdayanis.

ᚠᚢᚦᚨᚱᚲᚷᚹᛈᚺᛁᛃᛇᛢᛣᚤᛋᛏᛒᛖᛗᛚᛩᚠᚢᚦᚨᚱᚲᚷᚹᛈᚺᛁᛃᛇᛋᛏᛋᛒ

No other body has developed such a wealth of knowledge of pollution or such a sophisticated system of purification rites.

We know far less about the rites of the Germanic pagans, but the concept of purity lies at the heart of Ragnarok. For though the old world is destroyed, a new one emerges which is cleansed and pure. Yet the people find the chesspieces of the old gods, for the new world is this world purified.

Other poems, "Loki's Flyting" among them, also bear the stamp of pagan concepts of pollution and purification.

To properly use the runes, then, we need to know purification rites suitable to their calling.

EXERCISE 10

First, calm your mind. Do your relaxation exercise if necessary. Dismiss all daily thoughts. When your mind is composed, imagine yourself sitting in perfect darkness.

In front of you is a single flower, such as a rose. It is closed tightly. You are dirty, though the amount of dirt should be spontaneously created. Do not plan to have a patch here or there.

A light from no obvious source shines down upon you and the flower. As it does, the flower slowly opens. While the flower opens, the dirt on you slowly vanishes.

When the flower is fully opened, you should be clean.

This is a simple purification exercise, consisting entirely of mental images. Even without training it is of some use because the difficulty of getting the flower to open and the amount of dirt at both the beginning and end of the exercise tells us much about how you feel about yourself.

Quite simply, those who can't open the flower feel withdrawn from the world. Those who cannot get rid of the dirt or see themselves as very dirty feel that way about themselves. Where the dirt is placed may offer a clue to the cause of these feelings.

This basic and interdenominational purification rite is very useful. If nothing else it is a ritual a pagan, a Christian, a Buddhist, and a Muslim can all do together. It also has several modifications which make it useful for more specific purposes. But there are other rites of purification which are useful for the runes and, more specifically, derive from the Germanic pagan myths.

EXERCISE 11

The powers of the runes wynn (ᚹ) and doerg (ᛗ) between them form an excellent basis for a purification rite. It is most commonly used for purifying ritual objects, but it can also be used for purifying yourself.

Before yourself trace the rune wynn, carving and coloring the strokes as usual. Then carve and color doerg with the center of doerg coinciding with the vertical of wynn. You should get a figure like the following:

Let the energies of the runes pour into you while you recite:

The light of day
the glory of knowledge
remove all stain from me.

EXERCISE 12

There are other pagan methods of purification. One of these comes from the Norse worship of Thor. Where Odin was a god of the nobility, Thor was a god of the free or yeoman farmer. In addition to his powers to protect the gods, he also had the power, through his hammer, to hallow.

Simply inscribe the hammer Mjollnir, much as Christians use the cross. Begin by tracing the ring, then the handle, and finally the head. As you trace the lines you should see the trail of magical light.

The head of the hammer should be thicker than the handle, but it will not be as thick as a true hammerhead unless you can trace very wide lines of magical light.

There are no special words to recite when doing these strokes. When you have drawn the hammer, though, let its power flow into you and feel it changing you. Then recite:

With Mjollnir's might
and hallowed round
I am purified
in peace and on battleground.

Below is an illustration showing the strokes to be made when calling on the power of the hammer. Variants of this would be to call upon the spear of Odin, the ship of Njord, and so on. This, however, is leading us rather off the subject of the runes, and is perhaps better suited to another work at another time.

Although Thor is a specific deity, the hammer can be taken as a generic ingredient in runic magic. The history of the symbol of the hammer is quite long in Germanic paganism. We do know that worshippers of Thor would make the mark of the hammer over their food before eating. The symbol was close enough to a cross that one enterprising jeweller had a silver mould shaped for a cross, but with an iron plug which, when fit, would turn the mould to one for the hammer of Thor.

The hammer would be inherited by Thor's sons, and before Thor was the deity Donor, who, like Herakles, wielded a club. The hammer is in many ways a generic figure.

EXERCISE 13

There is one last exercise of purification. In a sense it is the opposite of all the others, since it requires an external source to allow the purification to work.

All you need is a bare patch of earth and a bit of solitude. The solitude isn't magically necessary, so if you don't mind being watched it's quite possible to do this rite in a crowd.

Simply stoop down and put the palms of your hands on bare soil, grass or other ground cover, or on a the trunk of a reasonably old tree. Recite the following:

> *Mother earth, mother earth,*
> *purify me by thy worth,*
> *take away every soul's stain,*
> *make me unpolluted again.*

PUTTING IT ALL TOGETHER

With all these exercises under your belt you'll be ready to perform runic magic. That includes not only spells, but astral projection and combining the runes in special spells. But before we do that, we'll have a second look at raising and using the power of the runes.

Note that this does not take any ritual implements. Though tools can be used, they are not essential.

Begin by dismissing all daily thoughts; you will only be concentrating on the rune(s) you want to use. All the parts of your soul have to be brought into line. Each of them must concentrate on some part of the spell at hand.

If any muscles are tensed, these must be relaxed. The tension will both distract from and inhibit the magic. If necessary, do one of the relaxation exercises and then try again to dismiss all mundane thoughts.

Your attention now turns to the rune(s) you wish to call. You will have already made this choice, of course. You will know the spell you wish to cast. And if it is a group of runes set as a monogram (see Chapter 7), you will have already decided how it will look.

ᚠᚢᚦᚨᚱᚲᚷᚹᚺᚾᛁᛃᛇᛈᛉᛋᛏᛒᛖᛗᛚᛜᛟᚠᚢᚦᚨᚱᚲᚷᚹᚺᚾᛁᛃᛇᛈᛉᛋᛏᛒ

Call up the image of the rune and see it in three dimensions, in detail, and with clarity. This focuses your mind on the project at hand and makes it harder for you to be distracted.

Only now that you've set the scene do you actually begin to draw the rune. This is done in the usual order of carving and coloring. With each stroke you say to yourself or out loud the recitation usual to the rune.

While you are doing this, continue with your visualization. This is often where people find difficulty, but visualizing correctly adds power to your spell because you're using so much more of yourself to power it.

To do this you have to split your attention. The image of the rune must be at the back or top of your head, as it were, and the lines at the very forefront of your attention. The verbal recitations take up another portion of your attention.

It is not as bad as it sounds: when we have a conversation and pour a drink at the same time we are splitting our attention. This is carrying the process a bit further and being aware of all the things we are doing.

So when the carving and coloring are done, the rune should be before you. It is then time to bring the image of the rune forward in your attention.

You can now manipulate the image of the rune in various ways. Particularly, you can see it bringing about the result you want. So odel (ᛟ), property, can be imagined as a chest with a lock on it. The lock looks like the rune odel.

When you open the lock, inside the chest are title deeds to property, or gold, or stocks and bonds, or however you picture wealth. You can even open the chest to find a house inside. Remember, the images are talking to your unconscious and do not have to be strictly logical.

This imagination and confirmation can take a bit of time, but it is worth the effort. The rune and its image combine with your variation to create an astral force which, once created, will seek embodiment on the physical plane. In other words, whatever you imagine will try to exist in physical matter with all its

ᛗᛗᛚᛉᛞᚠᚾᚦᚠᚱᚲᚷᛈᚺᛏᛁᚴᛊᛣᛦᛊᛏᛒᛗᛗᛚᛉᛞᚠᚾᚦᚠᚱᚲᚷᛈᚺᛏᛁᛊ

strength. The use of magical training and symbols helps provide for that greater strength.

The final stage is to recite a poem or statement which affirms that what you want to occur will happen. It is often assumed that such a statement has to be in Old Norse or some such language. Not so. Modern English does perfectly well, with the single exception that individual gods are addressed as "thee" rather than the more ambiguous "you," and the possessive is "thy" or "thine" rather than "your."

Again, if we're using odel to gain wealth we might use the following statement to cap the spell:

> I *am [name] and this is my wish,*
> *to have the wealth which I seek,*
> *in land and cash, and bullion of gold,*
> *to have a million within two hundred week.*

Though this example (becoming a millionaire in about four years) actually does rhyme, there is nothing essential about this. Apart from sounding nicer, it is easier to remember verse than prose. And there is nothing worse in a spell than not being able to remember what comes next.

You then need to end the spell so it can get to work. Giving thanks to the associated deity of the rune is excellent for this. In the case of the above example:

> *I thank thee, Var of the oath,*
> *who ensures fidelity,*
> *who grants all their ancestral rights.*
> *I grant to thee that the money I receive*
> *shall be inherited by all mine children.*

In that thanksgiving I have included the sacrifice. I have waited until now to mention it because it can be done in many places in the rite. A physical gift, for example, can be given before the rite is done and then mentioned in the thanksgiving. Or it can be given following relaxation when the image of the rune is being developed in your mind.

ᚠᚢᚦᚨᚱᚲᚷᚹᚺᚾᛁᛃᛇᛈᛉᛊᛏᛒᛖᛘᛚᛜᛞᚠᚢᚦᚨᚱᚲᚷᚹᚺᚾᛁᛃᛇᛈᛉᛊᛏᛒ

When to offer the gift is a choice which is highly personal, and any advice is only based on guesswork. I feel most comfortable with the gift coming first. Others have different opinions and should follow their inclinations.

There is an alternative to the thanksgiving style of closing. This is to, in the name of the associated deity, dismiss the powers of the rune to do their work. Then the final statement might go as follows:

> *Go to your task, rune odel,*
> *with Var's name I dismiss you from my sight,*
> *to go out and do that task with which you are charged.*
> *Thus it shall be.*

Again, the gift can be placed where you like in the ritual. But there is more to this magic than changing your life. To my mind a far greater power, and a greater evidence of the value of the runes than any spell, is astral projection. It is only now, after the long exercises you have done, that you can be considered ready for this practice. It is to that practice we turn next.

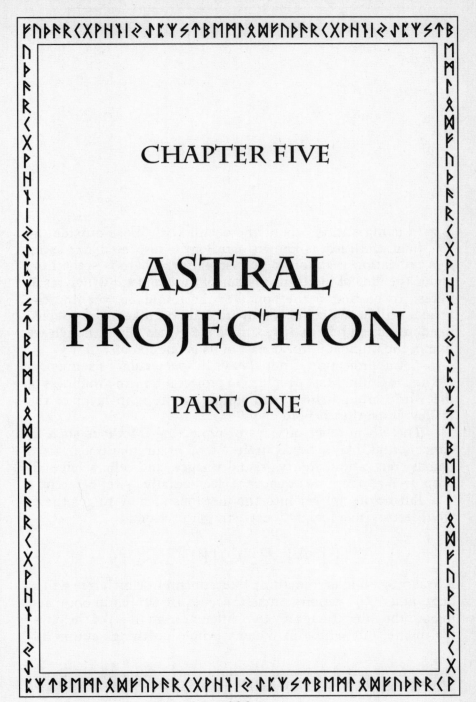

CHAPTER FIVE

ASTRAL PROJECTION

PART ONE

In conversations about the occult with those outside the field, the Tarot is known, astrology is respected, and astral projection is found to be fascinating. There is something about the idea of instilling visions of the fantastic which fascinates. To be free of the bonds of the mundane, yet find the visions still have a connection with reality, evokes a deep-seated need in human beings. It's as if we are aware that although we live in the mundane world, part of us is not actually of it.

Astral projection is not always as spectacular as some people might think. Most people who project retain an awareness of the world around them, and simply ignore it in favor of the vision which they behold.

There a number of ways of projecting. Methods such as dance, drugs, plays, deprivation of food or air, mantras, music, rituals, relaxation, injury, visual images, and others have all been used at one time or another, accidentally or deliberately.

But before we get into the methods of how to get there, we'll start with a look at what astral projection is.

ASTRAL PROJECTION

Astral projection is something like a dream in which free will is kept intact. The various fantastic scenes are similar in both, and in both the inhabitants are often different from those of the physical plane. But where in dreams people do things autonomically—without thought or choice—in astral projection they retain their whole consciousness. They can mull things over, make reasoned decisions, and understand cause and effect.

But astral projection is far more than human imagination given free play. Or to put it another way, the human imagination is far more than we give it credit for.

When you astrally project you are still subject to natural laws. These may be far more flexible than those we're used to, but they still exist. The experience is still part of a real world, just not the world we know.

This is so much so that some practitioners of the art can travel knowledgably on the astral plane. Two such people can knowingly astrally project, travel to the same place, exchange information, and then return to their physical bodies with the memory of that exchange intact. This, however, is the very apogee of the art.

What is more common, and what gives astral projection much of its value, is that the nature of the experience can be controlled to at least a small degree ahead of time. There are two means of doing this, though in all the books I've read only one is ever mentioned.

The one that is mentioned is the use of the astral key. This is usually a visual image, like a red equilateral triangle, but it can be sound (mantra or spell) or any of the other devices used to gain access to the astral worlds.

A person who projects into the red triangle (called tejas) has an experience consistent with the element of fire. If the person were to project into the element of water (a silver crescent on its back), then the principles of that element would guide the experiences of that person on that trip.

It is possible to project astrally without a key or control. This was done quite often in the latter part of the nineteenth century. Spiritualists at seances would often have a crystal ball. As they stared into the crystal, they sometimes felt a strange sucking sensation. Those involved would feel as if they were being sucked into the crystal ball.

ᛗᛗᛚ ᚷᛗᚠᚾᚦᚠᚱ ᚲᚷᛈᚺᛉᛁ ᚧ ᛋᚲᚤ ᛋᛏᛒᛗᛗᛚ ᚷᛗᚠᚾᚦᚠᚱ ᚲᚷᛈᚺᛉᛁ ᚧ ᛋ

They would then project randomly into some part of the astral world. What part they couldn't tell, and description indicates it differed with every projection. But such practice is hardly useful and in some circumstances can even be dangerous.

The other method of guiding the projection, however, is by ritual magic. A spell beforehand will guide the projection. The part of the astral plane into which you project is guided by the key, but the experiences of the projection are guided by the ritual.

This projection can be one or many. You can tie different astral projections together by this method. Thus, instead of 22 projections into the trumps of the Tarot, you can link them all to the meaning of the rite. Likewise the I Ching, runes, and other groups of keys can be linked for projection.

What you have then is an extremely powerful magical tool for spiritual advancement. The ritual creates, in effect, a geas or quest which you the magician fulfill (or fail to fulfill) by your actions in the projections.

You don't have to go through all the keys in one session. The projections can be spaced over a moderate period of time—a matter of days—but they will have a high degree of continuity in your experience.

The level of the continuity differs from one set of keys to another. But what is fascinating is how the experience of the key is consonant with the doorway used. People who use the keys to enter the elemental world of fire have an experience consonant with that key. People who use the runes have experiences consonant with the runes.

With that in mind, we'll take a second look at the keys.

THE ASTRAL KEYS

As we've mentioned, there are a multitude of astral keys. They are based on color, shape, sound, dance, drugs, plays, and more. It is the visual key that is most common, the sound key second; plays have been abandoned, and drugs have serious consequences.

We'll start with the less familiar keys. Plays were used in the Eleusinian mysteries. There the candidate, following preparation, would be taken into a cave. He or she would be left in silence and darkness until sensory deprivation began to take place.

Then lights would come on as oil lamps were lit. On a stage, actors would perform the play of the abduction of Proserpine. The combination of consistent meditation on the principles of the initiation, the exhaustion from the long progresses, the sensory deprivation, and the play would combine to take the candidate out of his or her body—he or she would experience the astral world.

Dance has been used by certain Sufi sects, the dervishes, for several centuries. Before them shamans used a similar technique of a whirling, hopping dance. The dance is performed to the beat of drums and the chant of the mantra. These lift the dancers out of their bodies, which collapse while they experience the astral world.

Sounds, in the form of chants, mantras, or spells, have long been used by Buddhists but are relatively uncommon in the West. Apart from some inferences in grimoires it is only Enochian magic and its keys or aethyrs which have really explored this method. And they are, in fact, spells, long pieces of text rather than mantras or chants.

The words of the text are themselves the means for entering the astral world. When the magician recites "Ol sonf vorsg, goho Iad Balt … " he or she is opening astral realms which since the end of the nineteenth century have been much explored.

Color and shape together in the form of symbols have provided the vast bulk of keys to the astral world. A full list would be impossible, but among the major groups used are the Tattwas, Tarot cards, and the I Ching hexagrams.

The Tattwas represent the five elements of spirit, fire, air, water, and earth, both in their pure state and in combination. Thus there are five mother Tattwas for the pure state and twenty sub-tattwas representing combinations such as air of water, fire of earth, or water of spirit.

In the Tarot, only the 22 major arcana are used.

And, of course, there are the runes. But these are somewhat different from the other keys, being bridged best by both a mantra or incantation and visual symbol.

When one considers the use of the complex symbols of the cities of pyramids in Enochian magic, a degree of similarity can be discerned. In both cases there is an incantation or chant which is correlated with a visual symbol. In both cases the various keys stand in definite relationship to one another. In both cases there is a guide or guardian to the keys. However, the relationships and the guides in the runes are very different from those in the Enochian realms.

THE RUNES

Each rune provides its own doorway into the nine worlds of Germanic pagan myth. The experiences you have of those worlds are different for each doorway. That is, your experience in gyfu will differ from the experience in ger.

But in all cases you will find the nine worlds. Countryside will predominate, and that countryside is consistent with the landscape of northern Europe several centuries ago.

You might still see a bear or a large wild ox (not uncommon in ur, in fact). There are wild boars, but these are not commonly encountered.

Winter is not uncommon, and the traveller will see snows. In other seasons the grasses and trees, too, are those of northern Europe. Mountain ranges are often found.

The beings one meets are also those familiar to the Germanic pagans. One does not find a sphinx or a winged angel. Instead, elves, imps, dark elves, trolls, giants, people, and gods occupy this part of the astral realm.

These do not always coincide perfectly with the images we have in existing texts. But it is true to say we don't know what ice demons looked like, and we certainly don't know the names of all the entities or what all the gods represented.

ᚠᚢᚦᚨᚱᚲᚷᚹᚺᚾᛁᛃᛇᛈᛉᛊᛏᛒᛖᛗᛚᛜᛞᚠᚢᚦᚨᚱᚲᚷᚹᚺᚾᛁᛃᛇᛈᛉᛊᛏᛒ

The differences and filled-in gaps should not be seen as errors. They can help fill in our knowledge of the Germanic myths—indeed, it was by projection that I concluded poerdh represents a funeral mound (previously unknown), and that the origin of the name of the rune was *perk*, meaning "to dig out."

Moreover, the astral plane is not simply fixed in a time warp. The Germanic myths continue to evolve today just as they did hundreds of years ago, and often things will exist on the astral plane before they come about on the physical plane. This, after all, is the basis of many spells and some prophecies.

There are some towns and cities in the runic keys, but far fewer than in the pathworkings of the Tree of Life, for example. The towns are more frequent, and are usually on the small side by modern expectations. The buildings have the high-pitched roofs and wood construction familiar to the Germanic pagans.

There are some of the characteristic long houses and pole houses, but more commonly there are individual units which house an extended family or, less commonly, a nuclear family. These villages are populated largely by men and women, but villages of dwarves and elves also exist, though these are rare.

There are also hamlets—four or five houses close to each other in the middle of a collective farm. And there are a number of individual dwellings occupied by hermits or individual farmers or woodcutters. It should be noted here that hermits were as known in Germanic and Celtic paganism as they were in Christianity.

The nature of these individual houses varies more widely. Some are wattle and daub, some are wooden. There are a few houses and forts made of stone. However, the more common use for stone is as a fence.

The wood in the houses is often pine but can be a hardwood. It is frequently carved and painted in the style of northern Europe.

Travel is by foot, or rather rarely, by horse. Travel by sea is in a variety of boats. Though the longboat is certainly known, it does not dominate. It is only used along rivers and then primarily by raiding parties.

On the open sea a wide-bottomed boat with a high prow and tail and a square-rigged sail is used. For river travel, merchants prefer a wide-bottomed but rather shallow boat with barely enough space in the hold for cargo. It's quite a sturdy boat, with pitch-painted hulls and a lower, often uncarved prow and tail. On these ships rowing is common, though those travelling the open sea rarely turn to the oars.

This description applies to what we might call the Midgard area of the astral world. There are other experiences corresponding to the other worlds of myth. There are vast castles of stone set in bleak stone landscapes where snow is frequent. This is the realm of the frost giants, Jotunheim, and the forbidding city of Utgard.

Giants and opposition will be found here. Giants do not like humans. Their furniture is sparse and frequently coarsely made. It is all set in proportion to people who are two to three times the height of humans (twelve to eighteen feet, or four to six meters).

Their common weapons are stones and clubs. Though they have metalworking—they have metal objects of decoration—they still exist in the Stone Age as far as warfare is concerned. They have no metal weapons, and I have never seen a domesticated animal or even a bow and arrow.

One can also travel to Asgard, home of the Aesir, and Valhalla, the hall of the slain where Odin still presses back Ragnarok. It is a vast hall where thousands eat. Its roof is a series of great black wooden beams; its shingles are warriors' shields.

The whole of Asgard is bounded by a great stone wall some 50 feet high. The houses are of wood and gleaming metal. Asgard has streets of metal cobblestones, and in this is nearly unique among all the dirt paths and forest trails.

The whole of the place has a warrior's air. There is feasting, singing, drinking, and fighting. In this respect Asgard is different from Vanaheim, the realm of the Vanir.

The Vanir are fertility gods, and their realm is not bounded by walls but by rivers, concourses, and waterfalls. The land has

ᚠᚢᚦᚨᚱᚲᚷᚹᚺᚾᛁᛃᛇᛈᛉᛊᛏᛒᛖᛗᛚᛜᛟᚠᚢᚦᚨᚱᚲᚷᚹᚺᛁᛃᛈᛉᛊᛏᛒ

no winter; crops are growing, ripening, and being harvested all the time. Its houses are humbler, and almost invariably wooden.

Poetry is more common here, and the people are at peace with each other. It is a pleasant realm, almost the opposite of Niflheim.

Niflheim is the realm of those who die ingloriously. It is a dank place of rotting—even gold rots there. There is a mist which is the breath of Nidhogg, the dragon. Nidhogg is so vast you can't see all of it, or even more than a small proportion of it. No one has ever seen its head. Its hide is glistening as if wet, and it is covered with black and green scales. You are so small in comparison that it doesn't even notice you.

Within the realm of the dead some whole plains or hall-ways are floored with animated corpses packed like cobble-stones. They suffer and gibber, writhe, and sometimes try to pull your down. Be careful around them.

There is a gleaming castle set on a promontory of a cave. This is the castle of Hel. It is here Hel has her chambers, with her glimmering bed. It doesn't react to light like other objects, rather its veils (like a four-poster) seem always to be giving off shadows from no obvious source of light.

She has two ancient servitors: a man and a woman. They look like standing corpses, but they are actually moving so slowly you have to stand and watch several minutes to see the difference.

Such are the kinds of scenes you will see. What will the experience be like? Several factors are common to almost all projections.

One of these is that you are given a role to play, as if you'd always been in this world. You don't arrive in jeans and sneak-ers. Rather you find yourself attired as these people are, and find you are a warrior, a magician, a merchant, a musician, even a noble or a serf, depending on the nature of the experience you will have.

In such a guise you will have the sort of equipment you will normally need. As a musician I might have a couple of instruments. As a warrior, a sword. A merchant has goods and pack animals. You will have what is needed for the part you will play—nothing more, nothing less.

This raises a question: are you yourself in the the projection? You are, for you have your own memories, your own personality, and your own vices and knowledge. But the environment and history have been changed. In this respect the runes are closer to the Enochian calls and to a lesser extent the Tarot than, say, the Tattwas or the I Ching hexagrams.

In particular, you are seeing a part of yourself, often a suppressed part, being brought to the fore. The experiences you undergo are often expressions of those parts of your personality which have been suppressed.

For example, if you have an aggressive personality you might project and find yourself to be a serf. A serf must show a great deal of deference since he or she has little opportunity to fight back. But this suppression of aggression now comes out in the form of a violent experience on the astral plane.

Alternatively you might find yourself a merchant because you are unorganized or unadventurous. Your experience would then center on events which force you into adventure or chaos.

A second thing common to runic projection is the existence of two guides: a lesser and a greater guide. The lesser guide will often be a friend or fellow traveller. He or she will know his or her way around the scenery, but he or she will not know the esoteric value of what is happening. To the lesser guide it is his or her world, and you are no different from any other inhabitant.

The greater guide is more likely to appear and disappear during your travels, but this is by no means a rule. Sometimes the greater guide will be with you the whole time, especially if you are projecting into only one rune.

The greater guide is not necessarily a god, although he or she may be, and often you are not certain of his or her status. He or she is aware of the esoteric nature of the world in which you travel, and is almost certainly able to know your true role.

Ignore your guide's advice at your own peril. It is usually short and cryptic, but will always lead you on the next necessary step of your quest or geas. Do not fight with the guide, since you will obviously lose.

The third common experience of projection into the runes is working through the nature of the runes themselves. It is possible to use some astral keys for more than entertainment. With the runes "a gift demands a gift," and you can expect each projection to demand something from you. They will test you, sometimes to the limit; they will make you work hard. But in the end you will be rewarded with the advancement of your soul, particularly in virtues of strength, loyalty, camaraderie, toughness, and courage. These are the experiences of the soul most common to the runes.

Finally, the projection into each rune is consistent with the nature of the rune itself. You will find physical objects or entities which are like the runes, and you will have experiences and tests to face which are consistent with that rune's meaning, image, color, number, etc.

You can also bind the runes together, projecting not just through one of them but through a series, including all of them. To bind these experiences together you need a ritual. It is this method of projection and that binding to which we turn now.

THE BINDING

Like the Enochian calls, to project properly into the runes takes not only their visualization but the proper use of the mantra. The mantra, or chant, is a single word repeated over and over to draw one deeper into the astral experience. The mantra is unique to each rune. But it is the binding of the runes together to unite the experiences into a single quest that we need to discuss here.

Binding is a technique that can apply to any group of keys: runes, Tarot, I Ching, Enochian calls, pathworking on the Tree of Life, even the Tattwas. It requires that a magical ritual precede each projection. Within this ritual is an oath stating the intent of the projection.

By performing the rite correctly, the magician charges his or her astral experience with the intent, with the oath, and changes the circumstances—not the surroundings, the circumstances—of the projection.

This, in fact, is not very different from using spells to change our earthly circumstances. If you cast a spell for money, you change your experience by ritual. In this case, however, you change the astral experience.

More than that, the astral experience then changes you. The series of projections becomes an initiatory experience. It changes your soul and, as all users of magic understand, a change in the soul will usually be quickly reflected by a change in circumstances.

With that in mind, we'll look first at the method of projection and then at binding together the projections into a quest.

METHOD OF PROJECTION

First, choose the rune into which you wish to project. This is not something which can be done casually, and some thought should go into the matter. For the same reason, you should be certain you won't be disturbed for the period of this exercise.

When you've chosen, sit in a comfortable chair with your feet flat on the floor. Your thighs should be parallel to the floor, and your arms on the armrests of the chair should be parallel to your thighs. Your back should be straight.

Seemingly running counter to all this is the alternative. You can use the ergonomic chairs which put you in a kind of half-kneeling position. These have the virtue of also keeping your spine straight and inhibiting your chances of falling asleep.

Once you're comfortable, you should shut your eyes and with will alone draw eohl before you, behind you, to your right, and to your left. This sets wards of protection. If you prefer, doerg or tyr can be used instead.

Breathe deeply and slowly a few times. Be sure to breathe from the chest, not with the stomach.

Imagine yourself walking the Bifrost, the rainbow bridge. This is a bridge of red, yellow, and blue material. This is not

ᚠᚢᚦᚨᚱᚲᚷᚹᚺᚾᛁᛇᛈᛉᛊᛏᛒᛖᛗᛚᛜᛞᚠᚢᚦᚨᚱᚲᚷᚹᚺᚾᛁᛇᛈᛉᛊᛏᛒ

wood, metal, stone, plastic or anything else you've come across. If you look closely you will find it's a woven material.

On either side of the bridge there are flames. Above you are the stars which are brighter than you've ever seen them. This is because, if you look down, you see the earth far below you. The bridge stretches from the planet to as far forward as you can see.

With your will, carve and color the rune through which you wish to project. Once it's colored it will move before you. As you walk you should, within yourself or out loud, chant the mantra of that rune.

It can sometimes lead you a considerable distance. Don't worry; it's quite normal.

When the rune does stop there will be a gate. This may be the gate to Asgard or Vanaheim or a gate at a stopping point on the bridge. With an act of will, pass through that gate and enter the realm of that rune.

When you are finished with the projection, summon the rune again and return to the rainbow bridge. You can then return to the physical world. Dismiss your wards.

It's a simple technique that can be aided by a number of tricks like self-hypnosis or white sound. But it takes a ritual to bind the projections together.

BEGINNING THE QUEST

The first step is to decide what you want to do in your quest. What do you want to discover about yourself? What do you want to change in yourself? What do you want to learn about in spiritual realities? What do you need to know to advance? What do you wish to do to help enhance the Vanir and Aesir in their work?

These goals can be narrow or broad, but they should be specific. A goal of "learning" is little good. Something like "why am I always afraid when I meet people?" is specific, concrete, and a good basis for a quest.

Similarly, "to know the value of courage" or "to learn my weaknesses and remove them," and even "to discover what I can do in life to strengthen the good" are all suitable bases for a quest in the astral world.

There are also quests to create changes in your environment. A quest "to learn how to get rich" or "to find love" is suitable. The quest here is similar to spells to achieve the same results. But there is a difference in that the quest not only seeks to bring about the physical conditions requested, but also to eliminate karmic debt and/or character flaws that prevent the quester from reaching that achievement or holding onto it when he or she gets it.

Once you've decided what you want, you can perform the ritual to bind the projections together. Several versions will work. This includes both rituals in other traditions and different rituals within the runic tradition. I would only warn you not to cross traditions between the runes and other groups of keys like the Tarot or the I Ching. I have learned from experience that the ritual for binding does not translate at all well.

Like most runic magic, the binding ritual can be done without paraphernalia. You need no more than your magical abilities. However, you can use some physical objects if you prefer, a matter we cover in the last chapter of this book.

Begin by finding a space in which to work. Then before you, behind you, to your right, then your left, carve and color eohl (Y) for protection.

When this is done, you need to purify yourself. This can be done in any of the ways mentioned in the previous chapter. You can also have a bowl of water and splash this first on one hand then the other. As you do, recite, "As a child is splashed with water, so I come to this rite innocent and new."

Next, you should make a sacrifice of a physical object or a change in yourself. Since the nature of the quest is such a change, I recommend that you choose a sacrifice of that sort.

For example, if your quest is to learn about love, call on Freyja and ask her guidance. Or you may include your sacrifice within your oath. This is the next step.

It is best to have the oath written down, for it must be said before each projection in the series. The form of the oath is quite open, but some requirements exist.

ᚠᚢᚦᚨᚱᚲᚷᚺᚾᛁᛄᛇᛈᛉᛋᛏᛒᛗᛚᛜᚠᚢᚦᚨᚱᚲᚷᚺᚾᛁᛄᛇᛈᛉᛋᛏᛒ

There must be acceptance of what the quest will achieve; this must be stated actively and concretely. The price paid must be set, though the acceptance of the change as presented through the projections is in itself often price enough.

But you must also address the gods or a god in particular as the patron and in some sense the binding power of the rite. For example, the oath below:

> *I stand before the gods of the Vanir and the Aesir,*
> *and before Odin, the All-Knowing, the wise.*
> *For I do not know myself as I ought.*
> *So I take oath with the runes, to examine each,*
> *that I might examine myself.*
> *I bind myself to change with the knowledge I gain;*
> *I bind myself to faithfully record my experiences.*

In this oath the reasons for the quest and the sacrifice to be made are both contained in the oath itself. Then state that the projection you are about to make is part of this oath:

> *Thus do I choose [rune] to teach me.*
> *It shall show how I shall [reason for quest]*
> *in the light of [nature of the rune].*

For example:

> *Thus do I choose nyd to teach me.*
> *I shall show how I shall learn of myself*
> *in the light of necessity.*

Then project in the manner we've given above. It is often advisable to spend some time chanting the rune to ensure the strength of the link. In this case you would combine it with an oath. Example:

> *With the power of [rune]*
> *I do continue my quest,*
> *to [purpose of quest]*
> *by the power of [nature of rune].*

This should be chanted nine times.

Thus this powerful magic can be performed simply, without a lot of magical equipment. The only bit of advice to remain

ᛗᛗᛚ ᛉᛗᚠᛝᚠᚱ ᚲᚷᛈᚺᛁᛇ ᛃᛂᛦᚤ ᛃᛏᛒᛗᛗᛚ ᛉᛗᚠᛝᚠᚱ ᚲᚷᛈᚺᛁᛇ ᛃ

is to provide the chant for each rune and notes on what sort of experience each will commonly provide.

THE RUNES

Rune: Feoh (ᚠ)
Chant: Freyfeohja
Common Experience: A festival, chance meeting, or other get-together.

Rune: Ur (ᚢ)
Chant: Urifew
Common Experience: Struggle with something, either an aspect of yourself or something external. On the astral plane the division is, perhaps, moot. Conflict with unresolved elements of the personality.

Rune: Thorn (ᚦ)
Chant: Draugrthorn
Common Experience: Severe test, karmic balance, often a glimpse of the negative side of your destiny.

Rune: Os (ᚨ)
Chant: Freyosodin
Common Experience: Meeting with the beneficent aspect of destiny; often the place where one meets the greater guide of the projections.

Rune: Rad (ᚱ)
Chant: Donrad
Common Experience: Sometimes a trip to the underworld, a meeting with death. Can more frequently be a meeting with change, including one's mortality.

Rune: Ken (ᚲ)
Chant: Kenfreyja
Common Experience: The experience of hope, of overcoming troubles in a seemingly easy way.

ᚠᚢᚦᚨᚱᚲᚷᚹᚺᚾᛁᛃᛇᛈᛉᛊᛏᛒᛖᛗᛚᛜᛞᚠᚢᚦᚨᚱᚲᚷᚹᚺᚾᛁᛃᛊᛏᛒ

Rune: Gyfu (X)
Chant: Freygyfu
Common Experience: The experience of balance; the indecisive will be faced with difficult choices.

Rune: Wynn (P)
Chant: Wynnifie
Common Experience: Secret knowledge, also piety. Wisdom, often in the form of sage advice.

Rune: Hoel (H)
Chant: Heimhoeldall
Common Experience: When projected into on its own it usually takes the form of isolation and loneliness. Will normally test one's resolve in some fashion.

Rune: Nyd (Y)
Chant: Nyddall
Common Experience: The experience of necessity, of learning to do what has to be done, to suffer what must be suffered, and how willingness to do this gets you through.

Rune: Isa (I)
Chant: Isaheim
Common Experience: The experience of power, often overwhelming power.

Rune: Ger (⬦)
Chant: Gerdolyar
Common Experience: A harvest, plenty, happiness. Those who cannot accept success do poorly in these projections.

Rune: Eoh (↓)
Chant: Eohdoll
Common Experience: The experience of the great, often in the form of secrets, and often in the form of the overwhelming.

ᛗᛗᚠᛉᛗᚠᚢᚦᚨᚱᚲᚷᛈᚺᚾᛁᚦᛃᛚᚲᛏᛋᛒᛗᛗᚠᛉᛗᚠᚢᚦᚨᚱᚲᚷᛈᚺᚾᛁᚦᛃ

Rune: Poerdh (ᚲ)
Chant: Poerdraugr
Common Experience: Being dragged down, loss, being faced with utter defeat or impenetrable barriers. What your life currently amounts to, but this may take a form you do not expect.

Rune: Eohl (ᛉ)
Chant: Eohlmanu
Common Experience: The experience of protection. Explores oath-worthiness.

Rune: Sighel (ᛋ)
Chant: Sonyal
Common Experience: The experience of transcendence. Projection into this rune leads to experiences of the value of the self as a spiritual being.

Rune: Tyr (ᛏ)
Chant: Tirwas
Common Experience: Conflict, honor, and justice; projection leads to a struggle. It is the justness and honor of the person protecting that leads to victory or defeat in the conflict. The conflict need not be physical, it can be an argument or simply a dressing down by one of the guides.

Rune: Boerc (ᛒ)
Chant: Boermanu
Common Experience: The experience of regeneration, which can take the form of a vision of rebirth, forgiveness, or cleansing. Can be powerful for the reformation of outer personality.

Rune: Ehwis (ᛗ)
Chant: Ehwitir
Common Experience: The experience of divine aid, rescue. A lesson that no odds are hopeless. Also the lesson of the immediacy of the divine in daily life. For the advanced, provides a view of the reason of destiny.

ᚠᚢᚦᚨᚱᚲᚷᚺᚾᛁᛃᛇᛈᛉᛋᛏᛒᛗᛚᛜᛞᚠᚢᚦᚨᚱᚲᚷᚺᚾᛁᛃᛇᛈᛉᛋᛏᛒ

Rune: Manu (ᛗ)
Chant: Manutir or Manunjord
Common Experience: The experience of self and species. Here the person projecting sees him or herself as he or she really is—not how the person sees him or herself normally or how others see the person, but how the gods see the person.

Rune: Lagu (ᛚ)
Chant: Laguman
Common Experience: Usually takes place at sea or on or by a river. Water will be present and be a dominant motif. It will show both sides of life (good and bad, rich and poor, etc.) to the person projecting. This can mean seeing what is being missed or that the grass is not always greener on the other side of the street. Expresses the power of the oath, which is what binds the two sides together.

Rune: Ing (ᛜ)
Chant: Ing
Common Experience: Community; will test the ability to hold things together. The experience of leadership.

Rune: Odel (ᛟ)
Chant: Odeltir
Common Experience: Wealth, family, property. Shows how the person projecting acts in this context.

Rune: Doerg (ᛞ)
Chant: Doervald
Common Experience: The test of salvation. The person projecting will be given a test which, if passed, will result in improvement in his or her life. If he or she fails the test, the quest has failed.

ᛗᚺᛚᛉᛞᚠᚾᛒᚠᚱᚲᚷᛈᚺᛁᛁᛇᛋᚲ� ᛋᛏᛒᛗᚺᛚᛉᛞᚠᚾᛒᚠᚱᚲᚷᛈᚺᛁᛁᛇᛋ

FINAL NOTES

The description of the experience is general because the runes can be very wide in their application. The lesson of the rune can come through experience or another entity. Some projections affect your mood, and some do not.

But in all cases you should take the projection very seriously. It is not an entertainment. One should neither enter merely to "see what's there" nor offer far too much for the vision—better not to pledge at all than to pledge overmuch.

CHAPTER SIX

ASTRAL PROJECTION

PART TWO

AN EXAMPLE

In this chapter I record a series of projections that includes all the runes of the Elder Futhark. It is an extensive record, I admit, but nothing less would provide you with an accurate picture of what can be expected in your own experiments.

It is a sometimes painful journey, and one more personal than I would have liked. Part of me wouldn't have minded if the publisher said, "Too long, we'll have to cut the chapter." But it didn't happen, and that is probably a good thing.

I want to show the power of this spiritual technique. Too often astral projection has been described as if it were spectacular entertainment, a stylized experiment in hallucinations without hallucinogenic drugs. It most certainly is not that. During periods of projections bound by rituals, such as this one, extraordinary things happen in life.

In my own case I found chance meetings with people I had not seen for months or years; reversals of fortune as that which had gone smoothly was suddenly upset, or that which was difficult suddenly went smoothly. In each case I could tie the event to a recent projection.

Dig deeply into yourself by this method and you will find your daily life being changed by it. More than that: when I projected I followed the normal alphabetical order of the Elder Futhark. The projections, however, follow their own order. If the story is given chronologically the projections follow this

order: feoh, os, ken, ur, hoel, etc. Yet the chronology fits perfectly, although the projections were (in some cases) separated
by days. This is one of the most extraordinary aspects of an
extraordinary magical alphabet.

•ᚠ•

Rune: Feoh
Order in Story: 1
Astral Projection: I project to find myself wearing a white tunic,
brown trousers, and calfskin boots. I carry a cloak for the nights,
but it is now a fine spring day.

I am some kind of minstrel. I have a staff to help me walk.
I have two instruments: a stringed instrument which seems to
be a cross between a mandolin or lute and a small harp, and a
wooden flute.

I put these over my shoulder and walk through the meadow.
I am by a creek but I head to the woods nearby. The trees there
are huge, and the moss on the forest floor is quite thick and soft.

I whistle a tune as I walk, since I am in fact unable to play
any instrument.

In time I come to another clearing. In about the middle of it
elves fight, a dark elf and a light elf using a club and a short
sword or long dagger respectively. I am reluctant to enter the
fight for, mythology aside, I know nothing of the struggle.

Eventually the elves notice me, and the dark elf voices his
disgust at a man being there. He challenges me, almost forgetting about the elf he was previously fighting.

As we argue, some hidden dark elves throw a net over me.
The light elf comes to my defense, but this amounts to no more
than commencing his fight with the dark elf again—the two
seem evenly matched.

The net is not weighted, and its weave is quite wide. I shove
my staff through one of the gaps and into the gut of a dark elf.

I try to thrust it the other way, but the net slows me too
much. I lift the edge of the net, taking a thump as I do. But my

ᛗᛖᛚ ᚱᛟᚠᚾᚦᛖᚱ ᚲᚷᛈᚺᛏᛁᠻ ᛋᚲᚤᛋᛏᛒᛗᛖᛚ ᚱᛟᚠᚾᚦᛖᚱ ᚲᚷᛈᚺᛏᛁᠻᛋ

staff and height soon give me an advantage. The dark elves run away. The last dark elf notices this state of affairs, and runs with his compatriots.

As we watch them go, the light elf turns to me, thanking me for the help, since he thought he might soon be in their net, himself. He asks where I travel, and I say nowhere in particular.

"Then do not travel that way, friend," he says, pointing to the dark elves' retreat. "That way lie many dark elves and they do not like humans."

"Why not?"

He shrugs. "They are dark elves."

I suggest the forest, and so we head in that direction.

The elf's name is Skirn, which means something like shining. It is an appropriate name, since the fellow seems to glow. I tell him my name, and he thinks "Jason" unusual.

"I am not from these parts."

He asks if I have learned a tune since coming to "these parts." I say I have, and begin to whistle it. He stops me, saying the tune is part of my inner self and I should not reveal it carelessly.

At Skirn's request I tell him of my world and its lack of tall trees and surplus of tall buildings. He does not like the idea, but I don't think he really believes it.

He asks what I'm doing here. I say I'm looking for the secret of friendship (the kind of self-knowledge feoh would most readily provide). So he takes me to the farm of a man named Hoenir, who lives there with his daughter and his cow.

Hoenir is glad to see us, and equally does not like the sound of my world.

"A man needs distance between himself and others before he can find peace," he says. As to friendship, he has an opinion of that, which he shares over his cider.

Friendship is like owning a cow. "A farmer gets a lot from a cow, and gives everything the cow needs. That's a friendship, and so long as the giving goes on, and so long as neither side gets too deeply in the debt of the other, the friendship continues."

It seems sage if rustic advice, and I say so—omitting the rustic part. Hoenir laughs, at which point his daughter walks in.

ᚠᚢᚦᚨᚱᚲᚷᚹ�губᚾᛁᛇᛃᛦᛋᛏᛒᛖᛗᛚᛜᛞᚠᚢᚦᚨᚱᚲᚷᚹᚺᚾᛁᛇᛃᛦᛋᛏᛒ

She is a plain, dark-haired girl. She carries a load of wood in one arm. She wears a worn white dress and has the dirt of chores still on her. Hoenir calls her over, with an arm around her waist he introduces her as Sigyn.

We drink, eat, and talk into the night, waking the next day with the sun. I'm mindful of Hoenir's words, and think of some way of repaying. I check and have no money.

Skirn reminds me of the tune I whistled the other day. I whistle it for Hoenir and Sigyn.

Skirn and I leave; I come back to this world.

•ᚢ•

Rune: Ur

Order in Events: 5

Astral Projection: (During the ritual before projection I find myself unable to put away thoughts of my experiences as a whistleblower in a government department. Nor can I turn aside the anger I have felt—and thought I'd gotten rid of—over those experiences. It led to a few newspaper headlines, but documents disappeared and there was little I could do in the circumstances.)

I emerge to find myself lying on the ground. I have a sword in my hand, a heavy thing which I did not have last time. (It will be gained in ken.)

I hear something, and turn to see the most enormous bull I have ever seen. It's rather more than six and a half feet tall at the shoulder.

I get out of the way of its charge just in time. As I get up my hand reflexively grasps a spear upon which I have fallen. The thing seems designed for boars, considering the broad blade and crossbar, and it's a bit rusty, but I'm not in a position to get technical. I clamber up a tree to get away.

The bull rams the tree, shaking it, and threatening to uproot it. I crawl along the branches to the branches of the next tree, then move along them and down the trunk. The bull wouldn't have noticed, but a pack of imps draws its attention to me.

ᛗᛖᛚᚪᛗᚠᚾᚦᚫᚱᚳᚷᛈᚻᛏᛁᛇ ᛋᚳᚣᛏᛒᛗᛖᛚᚪᛗᚠᚾᚦᚫᚱᚳᚷᛈᚻᛏᛁᛇᛋ

A continuing struggle of trying to smack the imps takes place. If the bull isn't attacking me, the imps are. At one point I drop my sack and the flute I carry falls out. An imp grabs it and runs. Despite the danger I chase after it, catching the imp and retrieving my flute before tossing the little creature away.

The bull catches me a few times. Were it my physical body I would surely be hurt more seriously than this. As it is, when the bull catches my left arm I feel it in my physical arm, which is first numb and then tingles.

I do catch the bull with the spear, penetrating to the crossbar. But I'm tossed off and lose the weapon. I notice the bull has blinders on, and can't see when charging. This gives me several chances to catch it with my sword, opening up gashes here and there. It works well until the thing turns in mid-charge.

I retreat up a tree to discover Skirn. I wonder aloud why the bull is so ferocious.

"Don't you remember? You wanted to cross his paddock. He had it all to himself until you said, 'It's a perfectly good path, he'll just have to let us use it.'"

I withdraw from the projection. It puts the question of whistleblowing not in terms of right and wrong—as I'd always seen it—but a territorial matter. Had I seen it as such before I would have handled it in a different way.

• ᚦ •

Rune: Thorn

Order in Events: 18

Astral Projection: I enter. It is suddenly cold. Skirn (the light elf) is with me, and he feels the cold as deeply as I do.

There is hoarfrost on the ground. It is fresh, though the day is bright and it should be spring. I wrap my cloak closer around me.

"What do we do now?"

"I suggest going some other way."

"The demon will catch us. It is quick," says Skirn. He does not sound fatalistic, merely factual.

ᚠᚢᚦᚨᚱᚲᚷᚹᚺᚾᛁᛃᛇᛈᛉᛋᛏᛒᛖᛗᛚᛜᛞᚠᚢᚦᚨᚱᚲᚷᚹᚺᚾᛁᛃᛇᛈᛉᛋᛏᛒ

"If he catches us?"

"He'll try to eat us. I only hope I shall die fighting."

From behind the trees comes the demon. It is perhaps the strangest such demon I have ever seen, and looks nothing like any other entity in Norse mythology. Not even anything like the creatures of Enochian or other styles of magic.

It is humanoid, grey with patches of lighter grey or white on its back. Its skin is a cross between leather and chitinous armor. Frost covers its jaws, and these are so distended by oversized teeth as to be almost mandibles. Its eyes are large, perfectly round, and yellow, without pupils.

Its forearms continue past the elbows in a kind of spike. This is not a weapon; tendons and muscles stretch over this, creating better leverage for the arm, I suppose. It wears an animal-skin breechcloth, but otherwise is naked.

So much might make biological sense. But its jaws are covered with frost, and its feet have a back-facing toe as well as five broad forward toes. I do not see how it could run on that.

For a reason which escapes me I wonder how much George Lucas would pay if I could catch the thing and bring it to the material world.

It suddenly leaps at the two of us. We hit the dirt, and when we rise the demon is between us and warmer lands. This, we soon guess, is its tactic. It knows it can handle the cold better than we can.

"Just keep backing up a bit," I tell Skirn. "It won't attack if it thinks it's still draining your strength."

I search through my sack. I find nothing as useful as a lighter, but there is metal and flint. When the demon sees this it snatches at me, knocking the things aside.

"At least we know it's afraid of fire."

"No good to us unless we get some."

We try backing in opposite directions, which upsets the creature. I cup my hands, mouth the Norse word *logi* (fire), and visualize a salamander.

On the material plane it's a good trick to warm yourself; here, an actual fire starts. I have stoked astral fires more easily in the past; it seems each method of magic must, even on the astral plane, follow its laws.

By the time the demon notices me, the fire is quite high. With this as a weapon I turn it around.

"Quick, run."

"No," says Skirn. "It'll just get other travellers."

I try to force the demon back. It leaps and climbs a tree. From there it spits at me, its spit a slush of snow and ice. It misses, but the ice would have hurt.

I dodge around the spit while the fire grows higher. I call on the rune ken, and the fire grows higher still. But when I call on that power, something inside me goes askew.

I feel, as close as I can describe it, as if I'd just had six cups of strong coffee after having no caffeine for a month. A voice inside me says: "Magic gained, magic lost, fire does not put out the frost. Order begun, order ended, from the magic deed more is descended. Find the path, find the route, if you find the secret all else is moot."

The demon runs away while I stand confused. I turn just in time to see a little man with glowing eyes. I recognise him as Loki in his companion or trickster guise.

He spins and disappears. I turn to Skirn, and he is as upset as I. We agree to press on to the House of Od.

• ᚱ •

Rune: Os

Order in Story: 2

Astral Projection: I walk a long time on the bridge before the rune stops receding before me. When I look down the Earth is no more than a large speck of light; a particularly bright star but only one among many.

I step in to find the house of Hoenir and Sigyn behind us. Until now I had truly wondered if the ritual would bind these projections together.

"Well, Skirn. To where shall we travel?"

ᚠᚢᚦᚨᚱᚲᚷᚹᚺᚾᛁᚾᛃᛇᛈᛉᛊᛏᛒᛖᛗᛚᛜᚠᚢᚦᚨᚱᚲᚷᚹᚺᚾᛁᚾᛃᛇᛈᛉᛊᛏᛒ

"You do not have a place in mind?"

"I came here to learn. About friendship. About what in myself I cannot control. And about the nine worlds."

"The gods? I have little to do with them. The Vanir are tricky, the Aesir are treacherous and violent, and the giants are not worth the land on which they walk."

"They have secrets I need to learn."

"There are some to whom you may turn for answers." He names several; Odin is not among them so I mention him.

"You are a fool if you think you can match wits with him."

"I don't seek to match wits with him, merely to learn from him."

"It's all the same under Odin's one eye. Perhaps you'd best look to another."

"Do you know of a place near here where we might go?"

"Not near here. It is a journey. It is the House of Od. He is a god who disappeared long ago. Freyja still mourns him, and maintains the house he first built. There are said to be secrets there, if one can plumb their depths."

We agree to go there, and begin our journey. We walk across a field dotted with trees. If we look only ahead, the tree line always seems to recede before us. If we look around, though, we know we are among the trees.

We are stopped by a large man wearing the most extraordinary belt. Even though he's a huge man, it is his belt of gem-inlaid lacquered metals in an intricate design and huge buckle that we notice first.

He bears a staff, wears a wide hat, and has an unkempt gray beard and tangled hair. He asks who we are; I introduce us.

He wants to know where we travel, so I tell him that, too. He finds it amusing. He asks me what I truly seek at the house of long-dead Od.

"He's not dead, just missing."

He leans close. "What do you seek?" I notice he has both eyes—this man is not Odin.

"What I seek I cannot put into words. Merely another step on an eternal quest."

ᛗᛗᚽᚷᛗᚠᚾᚦᚠᚱᚲᚷᛈᚺᛉᛁ᛬ᛖᛃᚲᚤᛋᛏᛒᛗᛗᚽᚷᛗᚠᚾᚦᚠᚱᚲᚷᛈᚺᛉᛁ᛬ᛖᛃ

"Such a fine thing. You want money, too, and girls." He taps my chest. "Inside you, you have never given up the hopes of youth."

I shrug. "I had a rotten adolescence."

He laughs. "And you are honest. That is good. Most deny the wishes they never fulfilled. They pretend they didn't mind loneliness, poverty, having less of a roof than a thrall. And yet I see no bitterness over this. No—something else."

He peers deeper, yet I find no intrusion to his examination. I think of rewriting a few bits of the conversation, I admit, but at the time there seemed to be no intrusion, no hostility toward me.

"Yes. The point of danger." He turns and walks away.

Skirn and I talk when he is gone. Skirn says the man had only one eye; I thought he had two. It could have been ...

• R •

Rune: Rad

Order in Story: 7

Astral Projection: I walk no distance at all before I am almost sucked into the world of Niflheim. It is a dank world, as if one were always walking in a tunnel. Throughout are the groans of the dead. Once in a while we hear the dreadful cry of Nidhogg.

This is a place of one's fears; one's hates. I have often wondered why rad was included in the first aett, but it seems to be a rune which makes you face things you would otherwise avoid.

The floor below me is spongy and made of packed corpses. In this world they are still animate, and some of them try to drag me down.

I have a sword, though I don't know from where I acquired it. I do not chop the corpses, but I am not tender when I kick their grasping hands away, or poke them with my walking staff.

Skirn is with me. He says nothing. I want to ask him how we got here and why we came. But the question would make no sense to him. He lives through these experiences with a chronology different from my own.

ᚠᚢᚦᚨᚱᚲᚷᚹᚺᚾᛁᛃᛇᛈᛉᛊᛏᛒᛖᛗᛚᛜᛞᚠᚢᚦᚨᚱᚲᚷᚹᚺᚾᛁᛃᛇᛊᛏᛒ

In my hand is a small metallic statue of a hawk. Without realizing it I had put away the sword and drawn this out of my bag. It is, perhaps, the means by which we got into this nightmarish realm.

"How much longer?" asks Skirn.

"I don't know."

"Well, are the hawk's eyes green?"

I look. They are brown with an iris of green. We press on.

We are met by a giant hound. Skirn throws it cakes, and while the animal is distracted we run around it. We hide as it passes by us, and I assume the smells of death have pervaded the place enough to blunt the animal's own sense of smell.

"Garm," I say, when it is gone.

We move on until we come to a door. The hawk's eyes are bright green.

"Do we knock?"

"We want to avoid attention."

We open the door carefully. Two ancient people stand in the room, not moving. These are Hel's servitors; alive, but moving so slowly that they are hard to pick from the dead.

In a tattered bed in the corner lies a figure. It is depressing to even approach the bed. It makes me feel sad, then tearful. Terrible thoughts well up from the terrible state of the world, to childhood memories, to other events.

I remember a little girl I saw when I myself was only a child. One side of her face was slack, unmuscled as if she had a stroke, though at the time I didn't know of strokes, let alone their effect. But this only affected her face.

She could not speak. She made noises to attract attention, then wrote on a pad she carried with her.

At the time I saw her I had a sudden stabbing realization. I saw she was as she was because too many people were so busy with their petty little ways of doing things. They were so busy struggling with each other over the inconsequential—sending planes to war or building buildings so they could open them and get their picture in the paper or having gala parties—that this girl was like this.

ᛗᛖᛚᛉᛞᚠᚾᚦᚠᚱᚲᚷᛈᚻᛇᛁᛉ ᛋᚲᛉᛋᛏᛒᛗᛗᛖᛉᛞᚠᚾᚦᚠᚱᚲᚷᛈᚻᛇᛁᛉᛋ

I was six. I swore then that I would change the world.

The figure in the bed is Hel. She is beautiful, pale, perfectly proportioned until your eye reaches her waist. Then there is horror. White skin gives way to pink and green and black, and maggots crawl in and out of sores.

I thought I would be revolted. Strangely, I am not. I am no longer even sad. I look back at Skirn, who is fearful. I toss him the hawk and mouth "go." I arch my eyebrows. He looks terrified, but at last, convinced I will do it, he turns and runs.

I turn back to the sleeping figure in the bed. "Hel."

She wakes. Is unafraid.

"I know you, Hel. I didn't think I did, but I know you."

"Who are you?"

"A man. Someone who made an oath without knowing the price."

"I do not free men from oaths."

She stands, perfectly naked, perfectly hideous in both halves. I would not expect to see Hel in a rune associated with Thor, but having done so I understand it.

"I don't ask you to. You see, I swore to build a new world. At six I swore this, and began to work each day to get ready for that event. But I didn't know the cost. I also swore not to become enmeshed in this world. I dug a chasm between myself and the world; there were bridges, perhaps, but still a gulf which people sensed. I made the mistake of isolating myself. People did not link well with me, and my network has lacked strength. I was too busy wanting to make it on my own, without help from or obligation to anyone. The result, I'm sorry to say, was exactly as it might be: the opportunities I had were lost."

She has perhaps heard the story before. If not from me, then from others.

"You have come here to disturb my sleep to tell me this?"

"I came to learn a secret. I have done so. Now I need instructions to travel to the House of Od. I understand you know the way."

She laughs. It is not pleasant. "Why should I tell a shaman like you? Odin himself could not get that information from me."

ᚠᚢᚦᚨᚱᚲᚷᚹᚺᚾᛁᛃᛇᛈᛉᛊᛏᛒᛖᛗᛚᛜᛞᚠᚢᚦᚨᚱᚲᚷᚹᚺᚾᛁᛃᛇᛈᛊᛏᛒ

"I am not a shaman. I study many magics. I want to know the way to the House of Od."

"Seek it as you will. You shall not wrench the secret from my lips."

I think of using magical fire, drawing on the power of ken again. Instead I let loose the light which itself is part of sigel, ken, and doerg. She flinches, but adjusts. The energy flowing through me is good.

"I cannot force you; you have more power than me. I cannot bribe you; there is nothing I would give up which you might want. But you are a daughter of Loki, and the snake has dripped on his face more than usual lately. Would it not serve your interests to tell me of the House of Od?"

"Why should it?"

"Perhaps even Odin fears the return of the House of Od."

She looks at me and refuses. After much argument I turn to go. As I walk away I see on the table a small object, gold, round. A globe. There is a falcon on it and two runes, os-doerg, Od.

I do not take it. As I walk on, Hel calls.

"Wait. Take the device. It will take you partway to the place you seek."

"Why give it to me? Why leave it there?"

"Perhaps it suits me."

I take the device. It feels warm, which is uncharacteristic in this realm. I thank her and leave.

Outside the door waits Skirn. We hold on to the falcon. It grows and flies with us on its back. There is spinning and we are back at the mouth of a cave. Half-eaten cakes lie next to a dog that has been tied to the mouth of the cave.

Skirn pays gold coins to the old priestess. We leave; I then return to this world.

• ‹ •

Rune: Ken
Order in Events: 3

ᛗᚪᛚᛉᛞᚠᚾᚦᚱᚳᚷᛈᚻᛟᛇ ᛋᚳᛦ�272ᛏᛒᛗᛗᚪᛉᛞᚠᚾᚦᚱᚳᚷᛈᚻᛟᛇᛋ

Astral Projection: I am holding a torch. It is night and Skirn and I have made camp in a clearing in the woods. On a wooden spit is a rabbit and nearby are some tubers dug up from somewhere. Some stones have been set in a circle around us; I am tracing runes in the air with the torch. Eohl is being traced over each to provide a protection.

"How long do you think it will take to find the House of Od?" asks Skirn.

"I'm more worried about that man with the funny belt."

"I think it was Odin. He seems to mean well enough." Skirn traces Thor's hammer in the air.

I finish tracing the last rune and spike the torch into the ground next to the fire. Skirn cuts meat for both of us.

In the distance a wolf howls. The night is crisp and not yet cold. The stars are bright and sharp, sharper by far than those over any city. The sky is not black but a very deep purple, and the shadows of the trees block out the stars in a great line around us.

"Which way shall we travel tomorrow?"

"Head along the same path. There's a cave in the distance. An old woman lives by it and is very wise. She will know the next step along the path."

"If she doesn't?"

"Use your magic." He goes back to eating, then stops. "Oh, but we'll have to take a detour as we go."

"No. We'll just head straight."

"There's a—"

"If it's a good path, follow it."

I remember the bull, but I also know in astral projections it is safest to follow the trail ahead of you. To step off is to get into trouble or even worse trouble. Besides, I know how the meeting with the bull will come out.

In the distance, beyond the reach of the fire, I see figures with gleaming yellow eyes. I nudge Skirn. He leans over.

"Imps, I hope. If not, they could be something worse."

I stand up and take the torch. The figures scatter.

"Dark elves?"

ᚠᚢᚦᚨᚱᚲᚷᚹᚺᚾᛁ᛬ᛃᛈᚴᛦᛋᛏᛒᛗᛖᛚᛉᛗᚠᚢᚦᚨᚱᚲᚷᚹᚺᚾᛁ᛬ᛃᛈᚴᛦᛋᛏᛒ

Skirn nods. I walk out into the darkness. I ignore his calls to come back. As I walk further from the camp, the figures surround me. In the light of the torch I see they are indeed dark elves armed with sticks and stones.

"So what do you lot want?"

"You."

"Me? What possible use could I be to you?"

"As a slave."

One makes a signal. I swing the torch, scattering them. As I thought, they don't much like the fire. The hair of one catches fire; screaming, it beats the flame out with its hands. One jumps on my back and is easily dislodged. I step back and keep them in front of me with the torch.

"Take a lot of slaves, do you? Keep many people in thrall?"

"Slaves make us strong. Make us rich. Make us strong enough to fight our enemies."

With the torch I trace ken. "Tell me. Where in the nine worlds do you find your place?"

"In anger. In hate. In all that breathes vengeance."

"I thought as much. Begone. I'll have nothing more to do with you."

"You will."

"I have already," I think. Then I turn to find them moving to attack. I ready, and find Skirn at my side as they press forward. Also there is the man with the belt; he gives me a sword.

"I should not like you to lose your way on your quest."

"I didn't ask for help."

"A man not willing to take help doesn't have many friends."

"My friends all have names."

"You'll learn mine in due time."

We finish the fight, which is not hard, since the dark elves are easily put to flight. I turn to the man again.

"Skirn is one guide; you, I take it, are the other."

"Indeed it might be so."

"So where is the secret here? What secret does the light hold?"

ᛗᚼᛚᚷᛞᚠᚾᚦᚱᚲᚷᛈᚺᛉᛁᛣ ᛋᚲᚤᛋᛏᛒᛗᚼᛚᚷᛞᚠᚾᚦᚱᚲᚷᛈᚺᛉᛁᛣ

"You've seen its face. Let go of your hate, and forget what was not a victory. Stop punishing yourself for what was."

He waves his hand and I am back. The secret here, perhaps, is forgiveness of oneself. It is not something I am good at. Perhaps it's time I practiced.

• X •

Rune: Gyfu

Order in Events: 4

Astral Projection: I project into the rune as if the rune were a part of the Bifrost, the rainbow bridge, itself. I emerge into the path I left, though it is the next day. It is the first continuity between two projections I have found.

Skirn is nowhere in sight, but as I am walking in a particular direction, I continue that path. I assume we agreed to meet somewhere or that he knows where I am going.

Though it was spring when we started, the grass is often yellow here. It is more like autumn than spring, yet the trees are just gaining their full foliage, and I assume that is the grass is naturally straw-like or the soil has a deficiency which the deeper-rooted trees can ignore.

A few times something catches the corner of my eye. But when I look, there is nothing. I ignore it, hoping carelessness will let me have a look at whatever is there. Perhaps there are imps, but it might be unwise to assume that.

I travel this way a considerable distance, worried I may have forgotten or missed something. I am assailed by doubt.

Where is Skirn? What will I do if I can't find him? I begin to doubt myself. Many thoughts tumble. Memories. Past failures and fears about the future.

Worse, I doubt what is real. The thiasus of which I am a member suddenly seems small and of no account. I seem so, too. I wonder about failures when I was working for the public service—that after two books of mine had been published I was demoted for a lack of written communication skills, complaints about documents missing from files notwithstanding.

ᚠᚢᚦᚨᚱᚲᚷᚹᚺᚾᛁᛃᛇᛈᛉᛊᛏᛒᛖᛗᛚᛜᚠᚢᚦᚨᚱᚲᚷᚹᚺᛁᛃᛊᚲᛃᛊᛏᛒ

I think of my marriage and wonder if it will last. What will that do to our child? Yet nothing endangers the marriage. Our daughter is growing well.

I slow, ready to stop. But as I do, I feel much worse. The slower I go the more the doubts come, the more things seem horrible, slimy, as if all is decaying in front of me.

I speed up. This eases but does not eliminate the situation. As I walk, my resistance to these doubts lessens. I begin to wonder why I bother trying. Nothing is going to come of anything I do.

I nearly withdraw from the rune before I guess that this is the secret of this rune. The secret of the gift is that it makes things matter.

I feel very alone. Am I not always the one who calls others? Don't I always have to arrange when to see others? They never come to see me.

I remind myself that's because I write. It takes a lot of time and they simply expect me to call when I have time for them.

I give them better presents than they give me.

You can't even tell your wife what you want. The only things you ever really want are books, and those have to be chosen with care.

So the debate goes, step by step as facades strip away. And underneath is a fear not simply of being unloved, but unlovable. That no matter what I ever do, no one will ever care. Not really. My parents didn't.

"That was then, this is now," I tell myself, almost desperately.

Then it all becomes too much. And I am surrounded by imps. Without a thought I swing, clubbing one. Then they are on me.

I struggle and swing my walking stick as they try to get open my bag. This is what they were after.

As they cover me the doubts get worse, and I realize the doubts emanate from them. It is their magic, their way of wearing down the traveler. But though I may suffer, I can always recover.

ᛖᛗᛚᚨᛞᚠᚾᛒᚨᚱᚲᚷᛈᚺᛉᛁᛇᛋᚲᚤᛋᛏᛒᛖᛗᛚᚨᛞᚠᚾᛒᚨᚱᚲᚷᛈᚺᛉᛁᛇᛋ

I call up the doubts and remember. Beatings. Loneliness. Worse. I had no friends for a long time, yet not long when one thinks of it. For it was my earlier childhood, not the later. I had many friends who overlooked faults I thought I could not bear to live with.

I was blamed, thought unlovable by the family that was left after the divorce. But I thrived in the end. Of all of us only I got the very great gift of doing what I want, to create words.

Without that pain I would never have turned to philosophy, and that was a very great gift.

And if friends don't call it's because I write. It's because they think I count enough to respect my creation.

No, I am not glib. I do not find conversation easy unless I know the person well. But most people are the same, and if it is a fault I can live with it.

I do not notice in the struggle that we have strayed. I look up to see Skirn travelling from branch to branch, keeping himself off the ground as much as possible. I assume I chose to walk, to test myself.

I turn to see, as expected, a bull. It is the imps' final weapon: stubbornness and unwillingness to change. It is very like the Germanic myths: a thing which cannot be defeated because it uses your strength to fight you. Like Thor fighting an old woman who turns out to be Old Age. The more I struggle against stubbornness, the less chance I have of winning.

Fighting old battles takes up energy. I break from the imps and run. When I am far enough away, I withdraw.

• ᚹ •

Rune: Wynn
Order in Events: 23
Astral Projection: It is night, though there are fewer stars out than usual. I look around the camp and see several figures, Skirn and the man with the belt among them. Someone puts a cup in my hand. It's filled with ale—at least I hope it's ale.

ᚠᚢᚦᚨᚱᚲᚷᚹᚺᚾᛁᛇᛃᛊᚲᚣᛋᛏᛒᛖᛗᛚᛜᚢᚠᚢᚦᚨᚱᚲᚷᚹᚺᚾᛁᛇᛃᛊᚲᚣᛋᛏᛒ

There is camaraderie here. The laughter is easy; people slouch in a way that indicates ease. They are in no danger.

A burst of fire reveals the face of the man with the belt. He has a bandage over one eye, the right. With his tangled gray hair, his beard, and his broad-rimmed floppy hat he does look like the image of Odin.

I remember that Odin gave up his eye for wisdom, and the rune I am in is wynn—glory or wisdom. It seems … enough.

I drink the ale. Someone calls, someone I do not know. A fighter.

"Jason, what will you do when we get to the House of Od?"

I see the legs of a woman next to the fire. I wonder if she is Freyja?

"Rest. It's been a longer journey than I would have liked."

All my life, I think. All my life and more.

Laughter goes around the fire. I look at the sky. I admit to being—not tired. Something in me has given up.

The man with the belt comes to sit by me.

"Where will you go after this? Travel more?"

"Probably. I have no path home, yet."

"You'll get there."

I shake my head and toss a stick into the fire.

"Odin." He answers. "Do you know where I mean when I say 'home'?"

"I know where you mean, and I know where it is. That you'll get there I can promise."

"After all the frustration in my life, all the things which have tried to draw me away, it seems impossible to believe."

"You let yourself be pulled from your path. But there's no blame in that."

It is easy conversation between friends. Yes, I'll make it. I should withdraw, but it's good company, in another world somehow still very much like ours.

• ᚺ •

ᛗᛗᛚᛉᛗᚠᚾᚦᚱᚲᚷᛈᚺᛉᛁᛇᛋᚲᛘᛋᛏᛒᛗᛗᛚᛉᛗᚠᚾᚦᚱᚲᚷᛈᚺᛉᛁᛇᛋ

Rune: Hoel

Order in Events: 6

Astral Projection: I curse the cold a few times; get up and huddle near the fire. Skirn grumbles, too. This is like winter.

I call on ken and give the fire a small magical boost. It does help a little, but not a lot.

Skirn, as unable to sleep as I, huddles near the fire, too. His fingers almost seem frostbitten.

"This is the breath of Hel. But the old woman who lives near the cave is the only one who can tell us the way to the House of Od."

I think he's trying to talk himself out of throwing the whole thing in and giving up. In the circumstances it doesn't seem all that bad an idea. But I've come further than he thinks and I won't be giving up this easily.

For an unknown time we warm ourselves, stamp our feet, and wait for the dawn. When it finally comes we are both exhausted. Worse, it doesn't get any warmer.

"Look, we'll make a flank. Try and get around the wind. If it's coming from the cave like breath, it should be coming in a stream."

We'll try anything. So we try walking around the blast of cold air. It takes us off the path, but it's a chance we'll take.

I forget something about the nature of the astral plane. It is a psychic realm. My actions and the world around me mesh in a particular way. The idea of a flanking maneuver around problems rather than meeting them head-on is a character flaw I have. If I can't meet it head-on, I try to get around it and attack it from another angle.

It doesn't always work, and I don't think about the chances of success before I do it.

In this case, we get out of the path of the icy wind, but we haven't gone far before we get to another problem. We're boxed in a natural canyon or crevasse.

"Go around it, or climb it?"

Skirn takes a look.

ᚠᚢᚦᚱᚲᚷᚹᚺᚾᛁᛃᛇᛈᛉᛊᛏᛒᛗᛚᛜᛞᚠᚢᚦᚱᚲᚷᚹᚺᚾᛁᛃᛇᛊᛏᛒ

"Warm up until we can stand the wind."

"That'd take too long. We'll back up and see if there's a short way around this. If there isn't, we can try getting on the other side of that wind stream."

When we try to backtrack we find the flaw in the plan. About twelve of them.

"Good evening, gentlemen." If that's what you say to a dozen giants.

They are about twice as tall as we are. Broad-shouldered. But instead of the rags I expected, their animal skins are well sewn into patterned garments.

"I really hate getting hit with a lot of things at once." It's an introspection; Skirn thinks it a flippant insanity.

"You wouldn't consider letting us pass by, would you?"

They make a path. Skirn is nervous, but I make my way through. Despite my expectations they don't turn against us. I soon find out why.

Some sort of creature on a leash is waiting for us. I have learned to deal with frustration in several ways. When they let the thing off its leash I use one of them.

I hit it. The animal, rather like a lizard, is not fast. It cannot turn. So with one jab it's blinded on one side. It is then that the giants turn on us.

With eohl called I set the wards. Their clubs and hammers miss. Skirn and I head back into the blast of icy wind. The giants pursue. With their long legs they keep up with us, and their swings keep getting closer.

I remain calmer than I thought I would. I concentrate, reinforcing the runes, dropping the ones ahead of us to send more magic to those behind.

Finally, I use ken to set a fire before us to keep off the cold and, I hope, to defeat the giants.

It fails. I am not understanding something here.

"Skirn, head that way; I'll draw them off. Don't argue, do."

Skirn runs off, and I turn on the giants. I call upon tyr, striking one down. As I do another swings his club. I duck, but get grazed by another.

ᛗᛖᛚᚷᛗᚢᚾᛒᛖᚱᚲᚷᚹᛈᚺᛉᛁᚦᛊᛚᚲᛦᛋᛏᛒᛗᛗᛚᚷᛗᚢᚾᛒᛖᚱᚲᚷᚹᛈᚺᛉᛁᚦᛊ

I see another time, another place. Another "giant," a child. I realize the frustration and purge it from my soul.

I was a child. How could I have won? I could not, and so I was beaten.

I turn my attention to the staff, and let it rise. As it does it carries me above their heads. Though they throw things at me, they miss. The fires I send back scatter them.

I land, and through the cold Skirn and I head for the cave. Shortly before it, the wind stops as if we are in the eye of a cyclone. We ask the old woman for her help, agree to her terms, and take the magical items we need.

I withdraw here, knowing we are about to enter Niflheim. The secret of this rune was simple: it was not defeating the giants, but being content with scattering them. I did not accept their value of victory or defeat, but imposed my own. I did not accept the standards that I was given, but rose above them. The runes through which I have traveled so far have already done much to change me.

.ᚾ.

Rune: Nyd

Order in Events: 15

Astral Projection: There is a force like electricity as I enter. It tingles through my arms.

I am in a larger group. Skirn is here, but also a woman and four other men. We walk along a path until we come to a promontory or escarpment. This overlooks a bay, and on one side of the bay is a village.

It consists of pole houses, one of which is a long house. There are perhaps a dozen other buildings in addition.

"That's them." I don't know the man who speaks.

As he speaks I see a flat-bottomed boat, with a dragon prow and a banner. The banner is a kind of quarter circle (oval, really) with a raven on it. Some green tassels complete the image. It hangs from a pole with an arm to hold the thing aloft.

ᚠᚢᚦᚨᚱᚲᚷᚹᚺᚾᛁᛇᛃᛈᚲᛉᛋᛏᛒᛖᛗᛚᛉᚾᚠᚢᚦᚨᚱᚲᚷᚹᚺᚾᛁᛇᛃᛈᚲᛉᛋᛏᛒ

"Odin's banner? Usually used by Vikings."

"These are simply raiders."

"I would have thought the village would be better fortified than this."

"That's because of the magic, Jason. It keeps them safe. But with your skills we hope to survive."

He grins. I grin back. Am I supposed to know a specific spell, or do they just think me that good? My preference is for philosophy; I don't even use divination as often as I could.

Skirn signals; I follow. The woman and one other man move as we do, but in a wider arc. The other three men lie down to watch over the escarpment.

"I find it surprising they don't have watchers."

"The magic. You still have Hel's globe?"

I reach into my bag; nod.

It takes us some time, but when we're ready there is one group of us at each of three points around the village. Keeping out of sight we settle down and wait for dusk.

As the sun sets everyone in the village gathers in the long house.

"What we're after is in there?"

"No. It's in the far house."

We head that way, making certain not to be seen. Skirn is surprisingly good at this furtive work, considering his shining state. Yet when I don't concentrate he seems not a shining figure but just like embers of a dying sun.

A kind of spell of invisibility. You see him but ignore him, explain him away.

We make it to the house at the end of the way easily. This is an ordinary house, except for the two guards.

We sit and wait. The man and the woman come around the side of the house.

Something alerts one of the guards. They look down the side of the house. They are about to raise the alarm when Skirn and I dash from the bushes. I strike with my sword but I only cut the man. Skirn is more efficient.

ᛗᚨᛚᚳᛞᚠᚢᚦᚱᚳᚷᛈᚺᛡᛁᛇ ᛋᚳᚤᛋᛏᛒᛗᛗᚨᛚᚳᛞᚠᚢᚦᚱᚳᚷᛈᚺᛡᛁᛇᛋ

The woman guts the guard as he staggers from the slash on the head. He falls in a heap.

Without a word we enter the house. There is a kind of shrine here unlike what one would expect in the north of Europe. It is a huge altar with decorated wood and gold. On the altar itself (which looks more Mahayana Buddhist than anything else) is a small object, a golden axe.

I reach for it. It feels like electricity is surrounding the thing. I look around; everyone is watching me. I remember what Skirn asked and pull out Hel's globe.

The gold gleams; the little falcon on top seems to move. As I bring it over toward the axe, it seems to throb.

A spark arcs between the two objects. I grab the axe without difficulty. With that, we run.

We get out of the house and are heading out of the town before we are spotted. People scream and chase us.

The three men on the hill begin to fire arrows at the pursuing crowd. We run into the forest with these people right behind us. They follow us as we scatter. Some of them bear torches, but most run headlong through the darkness.

One catches up to me and shouts that he's found the axe. I stab him while he's yelling, and run. But the crowd's heard him and is after me now.

It is dark enough that they can only get a fix on me by luck. As they do, however, they draw the others. My partners cut away at them, hitting their flanks again and again without mercy.

In time we get away. Regroup. The woman takes me to a place which must have been set up beforehand. We all get back.

The woman takes the axe; turns it over in her hands.

"With this the House of Od can be found in days. We are almost there."

I think that is optimistic.

"Could we have found the house without it?"

"Possibly. But without this key we could not have entered it. And only when we get inside will we learn the secret we've pledged to discover."

ᚠᚢ�þᚱᚲᚷᚹᚺᚾᛁᛃᛇᛈᛉᛋᛏᛒᛖᛗᛚᛜᚩᚠᚢᚦᚱᚲᚷᚺᚾᛁᛃᛇᛋᛏᛁᛋᛏᛒ

"It seems cruel to those people."

"They've killed enough, and used this axe to do it. They've killed people as if they were cattle for the sacred meal."

"What next?"

"We'll unleash its power tomorrow, Jason. It will show us the way."

"Why not get direction tonight?"

"Leave Freyja alone, Jason. She knows how to use the axe."

We settle down to camp. I withdraw.

• | •

Rune: Isa

Order in Events: 8

Astral Projection: "You have the globe?"

I'm still looking at it. The man with the belt is standing, staff in hand. I raise the globe so he can see it.

"I knew Hel would not give it to someone she thought could succeed. She does not want the House of Od discovered. He was always too much for life."

"Disliked each other, did they?"

"They never met. He disappeared before Loki bore her."

I know the myth. In the form of a mare Loki got pregnant and bore three children: Fenrir the wolf, Nidhogg the dragon, and Hel.

"What do you plan to do now?"

"Well, Skirn. You're the expert on this thing. What do we do with it?"

"We have to head north, north of Jotunheim. There the globe will show us the way."

"To the House of Od?"

"No, to the device which can show us the next step."

We set out, but the man with the belt does not accompany us. It doesn't take much travel to reach a roadside.

"We must be near a town."

"You are."

ᛗᛗᛚᚷᛗᚠᚢᚦᚱᚲᚷᛈᚺᛏᛁᚱᛋᛚᚲᚤᛋᛏᛒᛗᛗᛚᚷᛗᚠᚢᚦᚱᚲᚷᛈᚺᛏᛁᚱᛋ

We look up to see a man on a horse—a warrior in skins and armor, horned helmet on his head, unkempt red hair, moustache, and beard. He seems in a very good humor.

"Who are you?"

"Thorvalder. Who are you?"

"He's Skirn the elf. I'm Jason."

"Jason. I've never heard that name before."

"My friend," says Skirn, "is a magician."

"Ho. Then do magic!"

He snaps his fingers. Two other men come out of the bushes. They are smaller than Thorvalder but still look as if they know what they're about.

"If you wish." I use a simple spell to make the right arm of one of the men sore. It's mainly hypnotism with a cantrip tossed in, and works on the physical as well as the astral plane.

"What is this?"

"A simple spell which, cast properly, gives you the edge in a fight."

Thorvalder thinks this is good. He invites us to have a drink and I don't think it wise to tell him no.

He takes us to his village. After the meal and the beer he shows us the skill of his followers, who are the residents of the town. They are good with spears; I am not. But they take my lack of expertise in good humor, even the man whose spear gets broken when the shaft rather than the head hits the tree.

After this Thorvalder takes Skirn and me aside, into his house. It is a simple one-room affair with a loft for sleeping. The roof is decorated, but not overly so.

He sits in a large chair, behind which is a pillar. In the pillar is a nail in the forehead of a bearded figure (Thor, obviously), and on top of the pillar are wings (the architectural, not the feathered kind).

This pillar represents the tree Yggdrasil, the support of the cosmos. Oaths are spoken on it at public meetings, called *things*.

"I was told you two were coming. The signs were right, and the old woman said a stranger would come who had been touched by the gods. You are the one."

ᚠᚢᚦᚨᚱᚲᚷᚺᛃᛁᛇᛊᚲᛦᛌᛏᛒᛗᛗᛚᚦᛟᚢᚦᚨᚱᚲᚷᚺᛃᛁᛇᛊᚲᛦᛌᛏᛒ

"How on earth do you conclude that?" He stares; I change my words. "What makes you think that?"

Now he laughs.

"You come with a light elf, you have the demeanor of a warrior but not the skill, you know magic, and the wand of the old woman shows there is great magic in your bag."

"So?"

"So? We're to come with you. We have to keep you out of trouble. Without us your journey will fail. So! Will you heed the gods?"

I nod and ask when we will leave. I sleep in the town that night; the next day five of us set off on foot.

"We head north of Jotunheim. You'll meet giants, I'm sure."

"Met them before, Jason. You'll find a few split skulls in my past. I've even met the big, hairy, dumb ones. Never fight them, though. Stay out of their way and they won't harm you."

We continue to travel north for some time. The trees begin to thin out; game gets more scarce. We enter a range of mountains, and on the other side we find a bleak and barren landscape.

"Let's not stay here too long."

"Just long enough for the magic globe to work."

We travel past a huge, walled stone city. Utgard, surely. We see giant figures on the horizon. But we encounter no one, reach the north mountains, and hold up the globe. The light strikes it; the falcon moves and points his head in a new direction. We follow it, and after several days, realize we are being led directly to Jotunheim itself.

"Can we go around?"

"No. We'll have to brazen this through."

We enter Utgard. To my surprise there are many humans here, carrying on trade with the giants. We travel without impediment until we get to the southern gate.

We are ordered to pay the custom on our sales. The guards don't believe we've not sold anything. When I explain, the globe catches their eyes and we are hauled before Utgard-Loki, ruler of Jotunheim.

ᛗᛖᛚᚪᚹᚠᚾᛒᚪᚱᚲᚷᛈᚺᛁᛁᛇᛋᚲᛦᛋᛏᛒᛗᛖᛚᚪᚹᚠᚾᛒᚪᚱᚲᚷᛈᚺᛁᛁᛇᛋ

He offers to let us go if we show wisdom, and presents us with three riddles.

"What has three eyes, two arms, and eight legs?"

"Odin on Sleipnir."

I read that one in the myths.

"What does sunlight do to dark elves?"

"Turns them to stone." Skirn would know that.

"What did Odin say to Balder on his funeral pyre?"

"When the House of Od is open you shall return."

Utgard-Loki looks at the man in the broad-rimmed hat. His face contorts with rage.

"By my word you shall be let go. But not unmarked."

The man in the hat is seized and one eye is torn out. We all leave; I withdraw.

Rune: Ger

Order in Events: 14

Astral Projection: It is a time of harvest, with the grain high and ripe. I am with the woman who has been in previous projections. She is looking quite happy.

"With the raiders turned away we've got a decent harvest, for once. It'll be nice to see children who don't look too thin."

Skirn is somewhere, playing with children. Thorvalder is having a conversation with a local girl, of the sort that is trying to lead to something.

"How often do those raiders come?"

"Once a year at least. More often if they can manage it."

"Why don't the towns band together to rid themselves of these people?"

She shrugs. "It'd take a lot of lives. Those people have that magical axe which protects them. So long as they have it their village is safe from attack and their weapons will always carry the day."

"We beat them off."

ᚠᚢᚦᚨᚱᚲᚷᚹᚺᚾᛁ᛬ᛃᛱᚴᛦᛋᛏᛒᛗᛖᛚᛜᚠᚢᚦᚨᚱᚲᚷᚹᚺᚾᛁ᛬ᛃᛱᚴᛦᛋᛏᛒ

"We didn't use weapons. The axe does nothing against fire, or magic itself unless it attacks them. That was your tactic and we'd never thought of it."

Someone calls to her. Her name is Freyja. She goes to speak to someone—a man. She comes back.

"We want to ask you ... it's a lot to ask. Would you and your band be willing to deal with these raiders? We'd pay well."

"I want the axe."

"But that was my husband's. It was for the village."

"You can have it when I'm done with it. I need it to find the House of Od. Once I've done that it's yours. If you wish, you can send people with us to be sure of my word."

"I'll come myself, and bring Donor with me."

"Agreed."

With that the projection is over.

Rune: Eoh

Order in Story: 9

Astral Projection: We are outside Utgard. The man with the belt—and now with only one eye—is bandaging the gap in his face. Everyone seems almost cheerful.

"What is the matter with you people? This man just lost an eye!"

"Better that than our lives, Jason," says Thorvalder. "Your honesty nearly destroyed us. Utgard-Loki has little use for quests."

"Somebody should have told me."

"I thought it obvious not to say overmuch. You are garrulous."

The man with the belt restrains Thorvalder.

"Jason is a traveler here. Where he comes from to go on a quest is sacred, and others do not interfere. Is that not so?"

"A belief more honored in the breach than in the practice, I think."

"Honesty is your strong point, but it is like a good sword arm with no shield. You may win, but only with damage."

And damage is what I fear, if I am honest with myself. Pain offers neither barrier, nor discomfort, nor discipline. But damage, the irreparable—this I find difficult to handle.

We walk south, following the guidance of the globe. I think of the man with one eye. I could never be as stalwart in the face of such a loss.

As we travel we fall into groups, the man with the belt and I in front, the others behind.

"You worry about the eye I lost?"

"If it's my fault, I have done you a terrible disservice."

"It was fated to be. There is no use struggling against that."

"I thought I understood necessity."

"You understand too much. When anything escapes your grasp you become annoyed."

True. "You know a lot about me, Odin."

"I see. I see better with one eye than you do with two. Test me."

I am on his blind side. I raise fingers—two, four, one, five. He is not even looking in my direction but he gets them all right.

"You have tried to jump too far too quickly. Others cannot follow as fast as you. Slow up and you'll go more quickly."

"Why are you telling me this?"

"You do not find it useful?"

"Very. But I'm not certain why you would help me."

"Friendship of a sort. You have a bravery I admire, a bravery to not quit against overwhelming odds. But also pity, for you have tried to be the overwhelming force. Things change."

"You mean I shouldn't try as hard."

"Expect less of yourself or you'll be in an early grave."

"There's a kenning; a sword as head of Heimdall and Heimdall's head as a sword."

My test doesn't phase him.

"It means trying too hard, always watching your back even when there is no need. Heimdall always guards, and a sword is always a weapon."

ᚠᚢᚦᚨᚱᚲᚷᚹᚺᚾᛁᛃᛈᛇᛉᛊᛏᛒᛖᛗᛚᛜᚾᚢᚦᚨᚱᚲᚷᚹᚺᚾᛁᛃᛈᛇᛉᛊᛏᚤᛒ

"How can I succeed at what I want to do?"

"You are succeeding."

With that I am back in my physical body. I did not summon the rune nor will the change.

• ᚴ •

Rune: Poerdh
Order in Events: 12
Astral Projection: I did not want to enter poerdh, but the ritual demands all 24 runes. So I project and find myself facing the dead. Animated corpses are standing, moving slowly, and to one side of me is Hel.

"I want the globe back."

I would give it to her, but I don't know if I have the axe. If I give the globe away I'll never get it again. This, magically, may be the choice facing me, the reason the projections have followed such a strange timeline.

"Look. You can have it back when I'm done, but without it … "

"It is mine. Return it."

"It's beginning to look like I'll win, doesn't it?"

As I talk I dance around, avoiding these creatures. The sword is in my hand. I swing. On contact something like electricity flows from the creature to me. It hurts.

I realize I cannot win in a direct confrontation. But there are so many that I cannot get away, either.

"Look, can we just talk?"

The creatures move in. They are so slow, and I can feel my chest constrict.

I pick up a rock and throw. I learn you can hurt the dead, but they don't care. They ignore physical damage altogether and it is only pain that gives them pause.

"Where are my friends?"

No answer. I draw the Mjollnir as a magical sigil. That gets them backing off.

ᛗᛘᛚᚨᛈᚢ�ᚦᚱᚲᚷᛈᚺᛏᛁᚨᛋᚴᛟᛋᛏᛒᛗᛘᛚᚨᛈᚢᛑᚦᚱᚲᚷᛈᚺᛏᛁᚨᛋᛃ

The ground bursts with hands. Mottled hands grab at my ankles. I hack, breaking fingers from the hand, hand from the arm. But for every cut I, too, feel pain.

"Odin!"

Nothing. Hel just laughs. She is indeed beautiful and I wonder what my sword would do.

I call on magic, not for defense but for inspiration. Boerc, doerg, sighel, wynn, each on an arm of gyfu. It works well when I'm stuck in writing.

I remember my days as a whistleblower. No matter what I did, I could not win. I had two books published and they said I couldn't write. They said I wasn't technically-minded enough to do a computer job and push function keys—I was the only one to include computer programs I'd written in the job application. I complained, offered witnesses to threats of physical attack and of documents disappearing, and none of my witnesses were called.

And always I thought it my loss. My pain. To mention it all was to be a whiner. So I bottled it, like the beatings I got as a child. Like the bruises the teachers somehow didn't notice.

I swore to record this faithfully. I have. Even my thoughts.

I plunge my sword into the ground. I cannot win. It is not always worth winning.

What I forget is, had I won in the whistleblowing, and had the aide to the Member of Parliament who had been cheating the system and those who removed documents from files been prosecuted, I would in a real sense have lost. I would still be in that department today, propping it up as best I could. And I remember some of the people against whom I struggled have been labeled guilty of improper conduct by a Royal Comission.

The dead move closer. So like the people in the bureaucracy. I've seen my friends, and they are jealous of me for having left. I am training two on how to establish an outside job, a line to getting out.

I feel the electricity burn through me. I laugh. So like the Norse, perhaps, to laugh at death. But death is only the opening of a doorway.

ᚠᚢᚦᚨᚱᚲᚷᚹᚺᚾᛁᛃᛇᛈᛉᛊᛏᛒᛖᛗᛚᛜᛞᚠᚢᚦᚨᚱᚲᚷᚹᚺᚾᛁᛃᛇᛊᛏᛒ

I take the globe and throw it as far as I can. Hel cannot find it; Skirn will, or Odin. And as for these creatures, they cannot drag me down if I am not here.

I withdraw, realizing the favor the corrupt of this state have done me.

• Y •

Rune: Eohl

Order in Events: 13

Astral Projection: A spear is launched, striking down the nearest of the dead. There is a shout as Thorvalder lands a heavy rock on another of them. Odin, eye bandaged, drags his spear from one of the twice dead and closes in on Hel.

If he is not a god he is truly mad. But while we're at it I grab my sword. I may be useless against anybody who has even the faintest idea what they're doing, but these things move slowly.

It hurts to hit them, but they are driven off.

Hell has a staff and she and Odin put on a display of fighting skills which everyone has trouble not watching. It is like the Chinese martial arts dances, only it's all ad lib.

Skirn runs up last; being short, he is not as quick as some others. He tosses me the globe. The falcon's eyes begin to glow and it presses the dead back.

I had thrown away my defense, it seems.

I push the creatures back with the aid of the others (why have I never learned the names of the two friends of Thorvalder?). As I do, they dispatch them to make certain they will not cause trouble again.

There is an acrid smell. I turn to see Hel with a spear in her. Her face contorted with pain, she seems to liquify and dissolve into the dirt under her.

I only saw such a metamorphosis once before, and that was by a demon. Odin pulls his spear from the ground. It is oddly bloodless.

"Thank you, all of you. How did you ever find me?"

ᛗᛘᛚ᛬ᚪᛗᚠᚾᚦᚪᚱᚲᚷᛈᚻᛁᛁᛇ᛬ᛋᚲᛦᛋᛏᛒᛗᛘᛚ᛬ᚪᛗᚠᚾᚦᚪᚱᚲᚷᛈᚻᛁᛁᛇᛋ

"Your little trinket hit Skirn in the head."

I laugh. We all do. When the laughter stops, I feel uncomfortable. "I mean it. Thanks."

"You'd have done the same for us."

Would I? I suppose. We gather together and head off with some urgency.

"The village is coming under attack again," says Skirn.

When we get there the village is on fire—well, two houses. The raiding party is carrying off goods, money, and people.

No one can stand against them; extraordinary things happen when they try to do so: blades crack and break, people slip, tree branches break.

I hold back. I try to remember the effect of a previous projection. What did I do? What did she say? Something about magic not used directly against the raiders.

No, wait. There was something else …

"Jason. Come on! Come on! If we can't win we'll go down fighting!"

With disgust I'm left behind.

Fire. It didn't do anything against fire or magic that doesn't attack directly.

I look around and find a big villager. "You! Follow me."

We run, but when I start leading him away from the battle he stops. Calls me a coward.

"Our weapons are no good. Their magic stops our weapons so we'll use something else."

"Run if you like. I'll fight."

"I am fighting!"

He turns back without letting me explain. I find another, but he, too, won't listen.

I make my own way to the burning house. It's built on poles, which would be perfect if I had someone with muscle beside me.

The woman, Freyja, passes me. I call her.

"Get in the battle!"

"I am. Help me send them off."

"Pissing on the fire won't help get rid of them."

ᚠᚢᚦᚨᚱᚲᚷᛈᚺᚾᛁᛇᛃᚲᚤᛊᛏᛒᛗᛖᛚᛉᛜᚠᚢᚦᚨᚱᚲᚷᛈᚺᚾᛁᛇᛃᚲᚤᛊᛏᛒ

"I don't want to put it out, I want to use it!"

Finally, someone listens.

"Their magic is against warriors and their weapons. This fire is neither. If we can roll the logs through the village ... "

We shove. Nothing happens. We get a few more people to help but we only send one burning log rolling. But it does prove that the idea can work if we give it a chance.

I sit down and concentrate. Summoning ken, I call on the fire to burn brighter. The flames fan, the house breaks up, and the burning pieces flow like a river.

I do not direct it toward the raiders, or even the path they're taking. I send it at their ships. As soon as the raiders realize what is happening, they drop (almost) everything they're carrying and run to get out of range. I manage to burn a few out—merely "in the way," not a direct attack.

Then I fall over. They hold me up and cheer, and offer us a place to rest until harvest. I withdraw, exhausted. But their offer is taken.

• ᛋ •

Rune: Sighel

Order in Events: 17

Astral Projection: With Freyja beside me, Odin, Skirn, Thorvalder, and the others watch as I turn the axe in the light of the sun. A ray of reflected light glints onto the globe with the falcon on top. The falcon's eyes glow green. Then it ceases to be, returned to Hel and Niflheim where it belongs.

"Now what do we do?"

They all look at me.

"You're the leader," says Skirn. "You tell us."

"We press on to the House of Od. But if there's anything ..."

"We've come this far. Further we shall go."

"Good." I use the axe like a dowsing rod, but to no effect.

"We're too far," says Odin. "We need to head east. That will show us the place of the House."

ᛗᛖᛚᚨᛗᚠᚢᚦᚨᚱᚲᚷᛈᚺᛏᛁᛪ ᛋᛕᚤᛏᛒᛗᛖᛚᚨᛗᚠᚢᚦᚨᚱᚲᚷᛈᚺᛁᛪᛃ

We arrange for a ship and set sail, Freyja keeping the axe with her the whole time. I find myself withdrawing from the others. As we approach land, Odin comes to me and mentions my quietness.

"Just taking my duties seriously."

"More than that."

"I'm worried if I will succeed or not."

"You will succeed in the way in which you are meant."

We make landfall and drag the ship on shore. We fan out in small groups: Skirn and me, Thorvalder and Freyja, Odin alone, the other three by themselves. I realize I still don't know their names of Thorvalder's companions.

We walk for some time in the autumn sun, gathering kindling for fires and checking the game. We will have to press east tomorrow.

As we travel inland it gets colder. I recognize the place and tell Skirn to leave the wood behind. He agrees: "You know of this demon, too?"

"We've met." I withdraw.

• ↑ •

Rune: Tyr

Order in Story: 10

Astral Projection: We are traveling south from Jotunheim. The men are excited as the globe takes us from one place to another. It has been a long journey, and spring has given in to summer. We have left behind the stony, barren landscape of the giants in favor of fields of grain.

But many of these fields have been left fallow. What wheat or barley grows does so in competition with weeds. We think at first there is plague, but the burned houses around us tell us this is wrong.

We are watched with suspicion. People glower at us and do not answer our questions.

"I think it's time we found out what's happening here."

ᚠᚢᚦᚨᚱᚲᚷᚹᚺᚾᛁᛄᛇᛈᛉᛋᛏᛒᛖᛗᛚᛜᛞᚠᚢᚦᚨᚱᚲᚷᚹᚺᚾᛁᛄᛇᛈᛉᛋᛏᛒ

"You'll delay our journey to the House of Od."

"Listen, Thorvalder, I'll bet what is happening here has some effect on your journey to the House of Od."

"What makes you say that?"

"For one thing, the globe is glowing rather fiercely." I show him the device. "And the falcon's head moves quickly with the globe, so wherever we are heading must be close."

We find out what's happening when we're met by a large group of farmers armed with shovels, picks, forks, and other makeshift weapons. We are told about the raiders, and after a talk with the others we agree to side with the farmers.

With Thorvalder and his men we look like a professional band. We're taken to the village I have seen before.

There we meet Freyja, the leader of the village. She is suspicious of us and wants to know what we're after. I look at Odin and to his nod, give our story.

"We're looking for the House of Od. This globe tells us this place is somehow on the path. We're looking for the object which can next show us the way to the House."

The falcon is looking at the woman, and she replies, "Od was my husband. He and I built the first house in this village. But after raiders came he went away for a year, and returned—I am not sure how—with a golden axe. He said it would protect us from any enemy, any attack, and any weapon. When the two of us drove off a raid by 50 men, word spread quickly.

"Others came to the village and we prospered. Until a few years ago. The axe was stolen by raiders who now plunder us at their ease.

"Shortly after the theft my husband disappeared, and has not been heard from since."

We sit down to make plans for the coming fight. Thorvalder asks me why I give our help so readily.

"Justice. I have little love for raiders, having seen more than enough of them."

• ᛒ •

ᛗᛗᛚᛉᛝᚠᚾ�473ᚲᛉᛈᚺᛏᛁᚲ ᛃᚲᚤᛋᛏᛒᛗᛗᛚᛉᛝᚠᚾ�47ᚲᛉᛈᚺᛏᛁᚲᛃ

Rune: Boerc

Order in Events: 19

Astral Projection: We return to the camp of the eastern shore, telling the others of the ice demon we have met, and Loki. They all have similar stories; have all met something which they had to face.

I apologize for leading them into danger. They howl me down.

"Where you come from must be cowards to never want to face danger."

"I've put us into—"

"We landed and scouted about. A few skirmishes now and then keeps us on our toes."

"Don't small things like the loss of an eye or confronting some kind of nightmare in the flesh bother you?"

"Not if the prize is worth the fight. Now, let us be off!"

We actually camp for the night, but the next day we begin to head inland. This is a wild place, far less tame than the land where we'd just been. There are neither people nor giants here.

"Dark elves live in this place," says Skirn. We all take note of the fact.

It is Odin who comes up to me.

"You still do not understand."

"About the eye."

"About these people. They are not like your people, always seeking to reduce risk. They want to test themselves; to stretch themselves. To take a risk as a chance to get the prize a little sooner. They measure themselves by courage, either in quests like this or raiding or simple daily life.

"You keep thinking that getting to the House of Od is the secret. The secret is the path you use to get there."

He throws the spear and splits a small branch on a tree.

"Such a description means I can never win. Achievement means just another test. Doing things easily ... "

"Wait. Win? Is that all that matters?"

ᚠᚢᚦᚱᚲᚷᛪᛈᚺᛇᛄᛊᚲᚤᛉᛏᛒᛗᛗᛚᛉᛗᚠᚢᚦᚱᚲᚷᛪᛈᚺᛇᛄᛊᚲᚤᛊᛏᛒ

"Winning honestly."

"It's still winning. An ending. These people always want to climb the mountain but don't need to reach the top."

"And I do?"

"You need to win, because you believe winning makes you worthwhile. You want to be safe so no one can overwhelm you again. What you need to understand is that the scale of things has changed."

"You mean I've grown up?"

"More than that. You've begun to tap your real powers. You are creative; you have pierced barriers no one has pierced before."

"Not a very big barrier."

"Do they have to be big?"

"One did."

"Three. There were three large barriers you wanted to pierce, and at least one of them shows signs of rending."

Again, I am back in my body without willing it.

•ᛗ•

Rune: Ehwis

Order in Events: 11

Astral Projection: "I want the globe back."

I look around. There is no one to cause the voice. I recognize it, though. It's Hel.

I'm in the village. At my suggestion the people aren't going to try to meet the raiders head-on. Instead they will hide themselves in hopes of flanking the lot of them.

I could perhaps have suggested magic, but this option seems to involve everybody and gives them a chance to try means normally under their control to solve a problem.

Once that wouldn't have been important to me, but things change. So do people.

The globe has been the warning system. As the raiders come it turns its head toward their ship, even before we can see it.

ᛗᛗᛚᛉᛗᚠᚾᚠᚱᚲᚷᛈᚺᛏᛁᛩᛃᛈᚲᛇᛏᛒᛗᛗᛚᛉᛗᚠᚾᚠᚱᚲᚷᛈᚺᛏᛁᛩᛃ

"We'll have to keep that after we get back our axe," says a villager. I don't know if he means it, but it might have something to do with Hel's voice.

"I want my globe back."

"When I'm done with it you can have it. You've my word."

"Word of mortals. What good is the word of men?"

"What good is yours if you do not keep it?"

"Who are you talking to?"

I explain to Skirn, who sends word to the rest of our party. We are on one side of the village, there to attack the flank of the raiders as they come up the path to the village.

They are so confident that they don't even bother with a sneak attack. We're hoping to change that.

The globe begins to tingle. If I do not hold it, it begins to roll away from me—uphill. I try to hold it back, but as the raiders storm up the path to the village I am distracted.

As it gets away I turn and chase it, being led off from the others. I hear in the background a voice calling me a coward; a woman's voice.

I follow the globe as it keeps ahead of me. When I finally catch it the village is out of sight.

Torches light up around me, and Hel is there. She raises a hand to command me, but her magic fails. This perplexes her—me, too.

"You have divine aid, then." she says. "We'll see if these silly little gods can protect you for long."

With that she raises a hand. Corpses burst from the earth; they begin to move toward me. It is then that I withdraw.

• ᛗ •

Rune: Manu

Order in Events: 16

Astral Projection: I project easily, and am in the village where the raiders have been chased off. The time until the harvest is spent in chores, getting to know people, and becoming lost in thought.

ᚠᚢᚦᚨᚱᚲᚷᚹᚺᚾᛁᛄᛇᛈᛉᛊᛏᛒᛖᛗᛚᛜᛞᚠᚢᚦᚨᚱᚲᚷᚹᚺᚾᛁᛄᛇᛈᛉᛊᛏᛒ

Lost? More like found in thought. As I experience in speeded-up fashion the time of summer I begin to gain an appreciation of what I am doing.

I gain rather more of an appreciation of myself, too, and see the journey to the House of Od in a different light. It is the path there, the struggles I have had, which makes me ready to come to this house.

I've no idea what I will learn, but even if it's nothing, the journey will have been worth it. Life is not simply a matter of climaxes or peak experiences.

Odin disappears for a long time, and others wonder why I am so sure he will turn up when the time is right. I see in them the doubt I saw in the faces of coworkers when I said there was something rotten in the state of Denmark, or when I said we were going to face another major depression.

Several times the economy took a dip and they asked, "Is this it?" I said no. Until I walked in and said, "Remember the depression I said was coming? This is it. It will last ten years."

I have not been swayed by convention, and must expect people to not understand that until I show that my variation from the norm is because of what I see.

I remember looking at the first space shuttle launch. I said, "They'll have trouble with this. It'll blow up in flight."

People didn't like me saying that. All I was looking at was the exhaust. You can tell the difference between liquid and solid fuel rockets. I saw the solid boosters and I saw trouble. The technology had pushed beyond its capacity.

Now my friends don't question my opinions of space exploration, whether it's on the Cape York Peninsula space base or Space Station Freedom or the trip to Mars we must take.

I look up from such musings to find Odin, his eye patched, his spear a walking staff. I understand much more of what he was trying to say. In fact, I understand why people have often wondered how I came to conclusions divergent from those of the experts.

If you stand against the whole structure of something, expect it to take time for people to listen. I always thought it would be easier. And I measured myself against the ease with which I had hoped to achieve things.

I had all the right arguments, but people didn't have the means of judging whether my arguments were sound or not.

"It's not easy, is it?"

He shakes his head. I look at myself, and find myself at peace; even where I've lost, I find myself at peace.

I gather the group and tell them it is time to travel east, because that is where the House of Od must lie. It is not a place of power, but of knowledge. I am not a person of power, but of knowledge. I do not order, I teach.

I remember Hoenir and his daughter, Sigyn. I remember the tune I whistled, a mark of myself.

We prepare, and I am ready. I withdraw.

• ᚾ •

Rune: Lagu

Order in Events: 20

Astral Projection: We continue east, following a stream of water. The occasional leap of a fish can be seen. There is excitement—I feel very close to the House of Od and a revelation great or small, something I will learn.

Freyja, whose feelings I can only guess, holds the axe, using it to guide our way. So far it has kept us along this stream. Since the area provides water and food in abundance and wood is easy to find, I have no objection to this.

We come to foothills, and follow the stream back to come to a vast pool within a plateau of hills. Though it is beautiful I think how rare (read nonexistent) such a formation is in our world. The streams pour into what looks like an old volcanic or meteorite crater, then pour out in the single stream we have been following. It seems our world is missing something.

We set camp. Several members of the group strip off their clothes and go for a swim. Odin, Skirn, and I do not, though Skirn eventually joins the others in the water.

ᚠᚢᚦᚨᚱᚲᚷᚹᚺᚾᛁ᛬ᛃᛦᚲᛣᛋᛏᛒᛗᛖᛚᛜᛞᚠᚢᚦᚨᚱᚲᚷᚹᚺᚾᛁ᛬ᛃᛦᚲᛋᛏᛒ

"Holding back again?"

"I usually do. This time it is simply a matter of being so close."

"You want to end the journey?"

"I want to get to the goal."

"Too quickly, perhaps."

"No doubt."

"What if you never reach the path to the end?"

"That's what life is usually like. But I'll try to get there."

"Not this quest—life in its entirety."

"Get to the end of that and you're at the end of the universe."

"As in Ragnarok?"

"I suppose so."

"Why did you swear to change yourself so? I heard the oath, and was surprised."

"Why?"

"It was painful. You knew it would be."

"But it would better myself."

"Most simply want to better their circumstances."

"That's their problem."

He smiles, seeing genuine humor in that. I reflect how there are no demons left—no monsters, imps, dark elves, or mad bulls.

"You sought to remove the darkest part of yourself the hardest way. Do you truly think that is common?"

"Quite the opposite. It's not common enough. But I had a great deal to work through, and I had to deal with it in a particular way."

"Your way. Your oath."

"Yes, I guess so. But is there anything wrong with that?"

We talk for some time more. The swimmers return; we bed down for the night. Just before I withdraw it dawns on me what the oath was.

It wasn't the quest, it was an older oath: that if I suffered so as a child, I would not knowingly let anyone else suffer like

ᛗᛖᛚᚨᛗᚠᚢ�‍�742ᚲᚷᛈᚺᛏᛁ⋄ᛊᚲᚤᛊᛏᛒᛗᛖᛚᚨᛗᚠᚢᛞᚨᚱᚲᚷᛈᚺᛏᛁ⋄ᛊ

that. It set me on a path to become the kind of person who would not do that. It was time, I guess, to accept that the effort had succeeded.

• ◊ •

Rune: Ing

Order in Events: 21

Astral Projection: Travelling from the camp at the side of the lake, we come to a walled village. It is not a common oppidum— a fort which doubles as a merchant's market with some houses. It is rather a village of several hundred on a hill ringed with trees which have been linked with logs, mud, and baked clay. This is a construction I have never seen or heard of. It would have taken years for the trees to grow into just the right shape.

The axe, according to Freyja, tells us to travel this way. But when we approach the walls we are told to go away.

Everyone wants to agree to the demand except Freyja and myself. Odin is silent.

"You didn't mind somebody losing an eye; you said you wanted to take risks. Here's a risk, and one worth taking."

"Risk, yes. Attacking a village wall, we're sure to die."

"I didn't say attack, Thorvalder. We simply have to get in."

He and and everyone else (except Odin) disagree, and agree only to set up camp while I go to talk to the people in the village.

"People. I have come only to talk. I bear you no ill will. Have you been attacked?"

There is no answer. I explain our quest. This at least brings a face to the wall. Somehow I cannot help but feel he will tell me my father smelled of elderberries and my mother was a hamster, but he doesn't.

"If you are on quest for the House of Od, prove it. Show us his golden axe, gift of the god."

"First you tell me why you are so unhappy to meet travelers."

"Do you not know there is a war?"

ᚠᚢᚦᚨᚱᚲᚷᚹᚺᚾᛁᛃᛇᚲᛚᛦᛋᛏᛒᛖᛗᛚᛣᛞᚠᚢᚦᚨᚱᚲᚷᚹᚺᚾᛁᛃᛇᚲᛚᛦᛋᛏᛒ

"I don't even know who there'd be a war with. We are travelers, recently crossed the sea."

He calls down; there is a sound of scraping. The huge door opens and I am allowed in.

Standing above me on his shield is the leader of the town. His name is Ingdall. His people are at war with the dark elves and their human allies. If they let us through their village they want the axe to protect themselves against their enemies.

"I have already promised that axe to another. It is up to those of her village, who have just regained it from raiders."

"You are not among the raiders yourself?"

"No. We got the axe back from them, then followed its guidance here."

For the first time it occurs to me that Od must have passed this way for them to know of the axe. But suddenly we are all friends, and the lot of us are welcomed inside.

Ingdall sets out a feast; I am seated next to his daughter, Sif. Like the goddess, she has long, blonde hair. She wears a green embroidered dress and headband. I ask her about the war.

"The dark elves have the upper hand. They have taken our outer lands, destroyed the crops, and hope to starve us out."

"There's plenty of food on the table."

"We have ample game, and the stores of grain will carry us to next harvest. But with the axe here we would soon defeat the enemy."

"That is up to Freyja."

I look to her. She is laughing, trying to press back the attentions of several of the village people.

"A decision she can only make at her leisure."

Sif nods. She has a word with an attendant and the attentions to Freyja settle down, if not actually cease.

I note the unusual structure of the village, and ask how it came to be.

"My grandfather's grandfather. He had a farm near here, and planted the trees in a wide circle around what was then crop land. When the trees grew large enough, he began the work of carrying the mud to turn it into a village. As he went on, others joined."

"Didn't he tell people his plan?"

"No. People only follow when you have something practical to offer. If it's an idea out of their reach they are not interested, no matter how good or great the plan."

Something to meditate upon, surely.

We finish eating and turn in for the night. During the night Sif comes to me.

"I was hoping we could talk."

"About what?"

"We must have that axe. We must ... "

"That's Freyja's decision. I'll talk to her; make a suggestion. But it's her decision."

"But you are the leader."

"Leader, not dictator."

She does not understand the distinction.

"I gave my word to her. I can't go back on that."

"You mean when you became leader you took an oath of what you would and would not do?"

"Yes."

"Most strange. But we must have that axe."

"You mean you must have victory."

"How can we have victory without that axe? They are stronger than us."

"You mean they *were*. Now we're here." I hope she believes that. "What's the war about?"

"They want slaves, money, and land. We want the land."

"You mean both groups have such numbers they need new farm land?"

"Yes. We crop it, or they do."

"Why don't you just split or expand in another direction?"

She gets angry; before she goes out the door she turns.

"Do you think we have not thought of that?"

I withdraw from the rune.

ᚠᚢᚦᚨᚱᚲᚷᚹᚺᚾᛁᛃᛇᛈᛉᛊᛏᛒᛖᛗᛚᛜᚠᚢᚦᚨᚱᚲᚷᚹᚺᚾᛁᛃᛇᛊᛏᛒ

• ᛟ •

Rune: Odel
Order in Events: 22
Astral Projection: I awake the next morning to the sound of rams' horns blaring. Men and women rush everywhere; the women are at the walls with the men.

I climb a tree to find that outside the village are dark elves and men, throwing axes and trying to set fire to the trees. The trees are living and do not burn, and the mud that bridges the trees will not catch fire, anyway.

But the enemy persists, and is trying to scale the walls.

I look around and see the leader of the village. Skirn, Odin, and the others have manned the wall and are helping to keep the attackers at bay. Odin, at least, never misses.

Freyja comes out a little later than the others. She is still clutching the axe when several men try to take it from her.

I grab the leader of the village and, sword waving, drag him with me.

"Freyja, hold the axe." To the leader (whose name I've forgotten): "You, too."

With both of them holding the axe I carve and color eohl and tyr and ing and odel. One by one the spells take effect, protecting the people and their property and giving them the power to attack. As I perform the magic, the village grows stronger. Our spears become more accurate; our axes bite more deeply. The enemy begins to retreat.

"Don't let them escape. Take them all as prisoners. Do you hear? Take them as prisoners!"

Only because their leader has obeyed me do they listen. And though many get away, many are caught. When I have them all together I make my point. "This is Freyja. She leads the village where Od once lived. They have lost many people to raids. But the raiders have been defeated.

"There is still prime land left uncropped. Fields now sow themselves but remain untilled, unharvested. If you are willing

ᛗᛖᛚᛉᛘᛄᚠᚦ� ᛋ 10195 ᛏᛒᛗᛗᛚᛉᛘᛄᚠᚦᛁᛣᚷᛈᚻᛁᛁᚴᛋ

to go live there in peace, forgetting all grudges, then there is land for you. Land you will own without debt to any person.

"Those of you willing can go freely."

It takes some time, but in the end the first of several parties is chosen to set sail back. Surprisingly, the leader of this village is willing to go, leaving his daughter to take over for him.

I am surprised how easy it is, once you actually get down to it. Our party is ready to leave, but the leader of the village has a parting word, telling us the story of Od.

"When he lost the golden axe to raiders, Od felt he had little to live for. He had failed those he cared for, and felt it was not the first time of failure. He could not face it again. So he began to wander, to find a place so inaccessible and so remote that no one would ever find it. On his travels he came here, tired and hungry. He was nearly torn to bits by the ice demons to the west. My wife and daughter tended him and learned of his life in his babblings. Learned, too, of the golden axe. We entreated him a thousand times to stay, or to tell us where he got the axe. But in the end he would do neither. He packed his bag and took his leave, heading to the black mountains in the east. It is there you will find his house, if he lives."

I tell him we'll find it. In the distance are snow-capped peaks which otherwise are black. We begin to head east; I withdraw from the rune.

· ᛗ ·

Rune: Doerg

Order in Events: 24

Astral Projection: We enter the mountains. The blackness we saw from a distance is caused by a flower, which is in fact a very deep purple. But the snow reflects the sun's light, so it is very bright in the mountains. Yellow is infused with the purple.

We trudge up the only path, assuming Od could not have walked any other way. Certainly not if he had only recently been battered by ice demons.

ᚠᚢᚦᚨᚱᚲᚷᚹᚺᚾᛁᛃᛖᛈᚲᛇᛋᛏᛒᛗᛗᛚᛗᚾᚠᚢᚦᚨᚱᚲᚷᚹᚺᛁᛃᛖᛈᚲᛇᛋᛏᛒ

The villagers didn't seem certain if he was still alive. Until now I had always assumed he was dead. I took the House of Od to be some kind of mausoleum or burial mound.

The path grows steeper and branches into three, looking like a giant rune of protection.

"Which way, Jason?" says Skirn.

"We could split up and check all three. The problem is what we do if one path splits again."

I think of half a dozen plans before remembering the axe. But when Freyja tries it, it offers no clue.

"Let me." I hold the axe, feeling the weight of its gold. All three paths show the House as lying along it. I do not feel that is right.

"Perhaps there are three houses?"

That, too, seems wrong. In the end I must make a choice, and can see no clue to guide me. Until at last the matter comes clear. "We'll go straight."

"How did you decide that?"

"Things have gone best when I've been direct. I'm assuming that is the underlying principle of the magic here."

To their consternation, I strike out straight ahead. I am guessing this is the nature of the test.

We travel some distance. Things seem to fade.

"Hold up!"

This does not feel right. The astral images become less—perfect. I go back and take another look at the paths. The left is the smaller, the one most difficult, and Od had been looking for the most inaccessible place.

But then, would he have taken any path? On the astral plane I have found that following the astral path is the safest course, but perhaps safety is not what this projection is about.

I start on the left path, but take no more than a step.

Everyone is wondering what is happening, and I feel the need to get going. I scratch the back of my neck.

My oath, to know myself.

"That way!"

ᛗᚢᛚᛉᛗᚠᚾᛚᚠᚱᚲᚷᛈᚺᛏᛁᛦ ᛋᛚᚲᛦᛋᛏᛒᛗᛗᚢᛚᛉᛗᚠᚾᛚᚠᚱᚲᚷᛈᚺᛏᛁᛦᛋ

We climb. We ignore the paths and climb the highest mountain. And there on the peak, tucked behind igneous flows of stone which have solidified, been weathered, and then carved, is a stone arch. On either side of the arch is a fire in a stone pot. The double doors within the arch are locked.

The golden axe is a key. I place it in the lock, turn, and the doors slide open. We all walk into the darkened chamber. Skirn's brightness lights the way.

We enter an elaborately carved chamber, with decorated ceiling and wooden bracings. Gold lies about the place in decorations and coins, so much junk to be swept up. In the center of the hall is a glowing gem. I touch it, and it is hot.

There are further chambers, but before we can explore them a man comes out. He is tall, muscular, and scarred on the arms and face; from Freyja's reaction, he is Od.

He almost ignores her. He looks at me and hands me a smaller version of the crystal in the room. It glows warm, and in it is a vision.

With the crystal are a few gold coins. I turn back to Od, and seem to be as small as a child. I realize I'm stooping, and straighten up.

To each of the others he gives a gift, except Odin. They seem to have met before.

We all leave, except Freyja. Skirn will take the axe back to the village. Thorvalder will look for adventure. Odin shall wander as he always does.

I have been given the nature of my quest. The vision was of myself; my spirit. The troubles and pain of a whistleblower are put aside. Another phase of life begins to open, and in that sense I—did not have to win.

ᚠᚢᚦᚨᚱᚲᚷᚹᚺᚾᛁᛃᛇᛋᚲᛦᛋᛏᛒᛖᛗᛚᛜᛗᚢᚦᚨᚱᚲᚷᚹᚺᚾᛁᛃᛇᛋᚲᛦᛋᛏᛒ

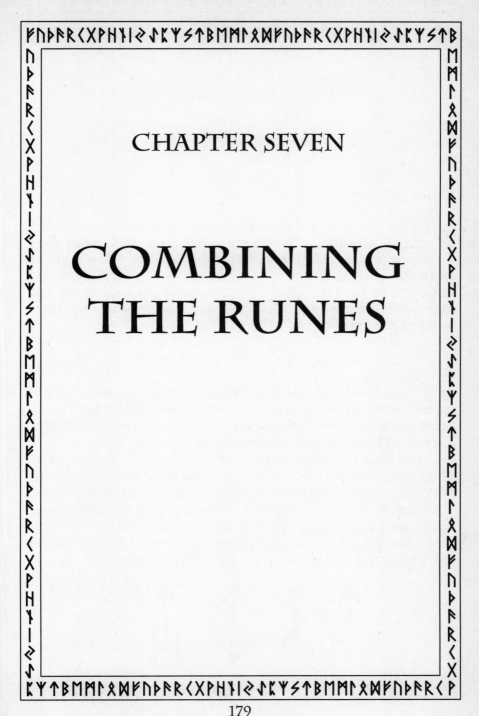

CHAPTER SEVEN

COMBINING THE RUNES

One of the greatest advantages of the runes over any other magical alphabet is that they can be combined to make their power more effective and specific. We are talking about more than stringing letters together into words, though the runes can be used in that manner. Rather, the runes can be put together to form sigils, talismans, and monograms with their own unique purposes.

MONOGRAMS

Runes can be superimposed over one another to form monograms. This was a common practice among the Germanic pagans, and was used by merchants to create their housemarks. They used these devices to identify their goods.

The principle of monograms is quite simple: two or more runes are combined into a single pleasing form by drawing them from a common perspective or with overlapping strokes.

Suppose we want to overcome the dark side of our personality. This can be expressed as tyr (for attack) and either hoel or thorn. Since tyr is to be triumphant, this rune would be on the top. This could lead to any of the following monograms:

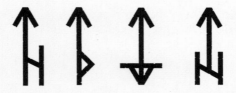

Monograms can become more complex than this, of course. We might want a monogram which means "I (manu) want the wisdom (wynn) to reach salvation (sighel) that the dark (hoel) be banished and the divine (ehwis) find me suitable for preferment (boerc)." In such a case we might get the following:

An alternative is not to choose runes by their symbolic but by their phonetic content. In this you take a statement summarizing your magical intent and write it out in full.

When all the duplicate letters have been struck out, combine those remaining into a single monogram. For example, "I wish to find true love" becomes IWSHTOFNDRUELV. When the letters are converted into runes, they look like this:

and can be converted into a monogram like this:

But there is more to it than making a statement, picking a few runes to fit it, and throwing them together. Like the runes themselves, the monograms are subject to the laws of esoteric symbolism. While simply combining the runes will have an effect, improving the technique provides a more efficient system.

A QUESTION OF SYMBOLISM

The top of a monogram, like a rune, is the position of power. The bottom is the position of response. The right is active (also called masculine); the left, receptive (feminine). The center is the point of becoming. This is all charted below:

Points of Power

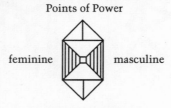

feminine   masculine

Points of Supplication

This provides us with a few rules for building up monograms for the best results. In constructing a monogram to overcome a fault, the rune of triumph should be placed above that of the fault to be overcome.

A monogram to receive wisdom or inspiration should have the symbol of the self on the left and the symbol of wisdom on the right. To express wisdom the opposite is done. So if we take manu (self) and wynn (wisdom) we would have the monogram on the left to receive wisdom, the one on the right to express it:

A monogram that does not conform to these rules still works, but it takes longer and the effect can be more muted. That is, light will triumph over darkness as part of the natural order of things. But if the monogram doesn't express this, it will take a longer time for it to happen in the specific circumstances of the monogram.

If the center of the monogram has a line through it, the monogram is a continuing force, one that does not end its influence. If the monogram has no line through the center, its force is limited to a period of time or to a specific event.

If the line filling the center is vertical, then it is formative power which leads to the becoming. If it is a diagonal, it is the structure which is built. If the diagonal is higher on the left it is passive exchange; higher on the right is active exchange. Passive exchange is unconscious or traditional. Active is conscious, planned out, and innovative.

Diagonals meeting in the center indicate an exchange in balance, one that has reached a stable state rather than the dynamic indicated by a single diagonal. A vertical and a diagonal meeting in the center indicate formative power having created an exchange, with the same rules applying for conscious and unconscious exchange. If vertical and both diagonals meet (as in the Anglo-Saxon version of gyfu, for example), this indicates a structure underpinned and relating back to the formative power; that is, the situation continues as long as the imminence of divine power persists.

You should take all these factors into account when constructing your monogram. Fortunately this is less difficult than it may appear. This process is helped by some conventions which make the creation of monograms easier.

TWO ORGANIZERS

A monogram can be built around a little central diamond called a lozenge. From the lozenge come four radiating arms, horizontal and vertical. In terms of the runes the two bars cancel each other out and so remain neutral.

This was a common device in medieval and Byzantine monograms. The one below, for example, is that of Charlemagne:

The lozenge helps organize the runes because it allows you to distance the runes from each other. The easiest way to use this device is to simply choose four runes and put them on the ends of the four bars. If we're choosing runes for ideographic rather than phonetic content we can safely repeat the runes.

For example, if we want to devise a monogram for both protection and attack we might decide to use tyr and eohl to do this. You need only put eohl twice on the horizontal bar, and tyr on the vertical. This would give you the monogram below:

If we wanted to protect our property we could use eohl and odel, and incorporate odel into the lozenge itself. We'd get something like the monogram below:

These monograms can get very complex. Below is an example of a monogram based on the phonetic values of the runes. The phrase used is "The blessings of Freyer upon this venture," or ThEBLSINGOFRYUPT. In this the T and Th are separate runes, tyr and thorn.

There are several ways we can combine these runes. First, we can amalgamate them so individual strokes coincide. This may get us the monogram in the following illustration:

We can use the lozenge. With this device we might get a monogram like the following:

Or third, we can place the runes on a figure of eight spokes. With this device we get the following figure:

When using these figures it's not essential to follow the strict letter of the rules. Remember, your understanding of the situation may be imperfect, so if your intuition or aesthetic sense tells you one version of a monogram is better than another, ignore this at your peril.

Indeed, there is no reason why the same number of runes has to be put on each arm of the cross or eight-spoked figures. If you wish to draw special attention to a particular rune or runes, these can be made larger than the others or placed by themselves on a stem. There is no special orientation to the runes: on these figures they can be drawn on their sides or upside down with no ill effect.

The stems themselves can be involved in the rune if they are actually part of a rune in their own right. Below is a monogram using gyfu as a central rune. It was mentioned in Chapter 6 as a monogram to derive inspiration.

ᛗᛖᛚᚨᛞᚠᚢᛏᚦᚱᚲᚷᛈᚺᛏᛁᛇᛋᚲᚤᛋᛏᛒᛗᛖᛚᚨᛞᚠᚢᛏᚦᚱᚲᚷᛈᚺᛏᛁᛇᛋ

Runes can also be used as generic inscriptions. Simply writing down an inscription in runes (or the Enochian alphabet) will help magically establish your intent. So we'll turn to inscriptions (literal spells) next.

RUNIC INSCRIPTIONS

You might think that all you have to do with a runic inscription is write it down in runes. There is rather more to it than that.

First, some notes on transliteration. Remember there is no "v" in the runes, so any v in your inscription will have to be represented by boerc. A "c" must be phonetically changed: if hard it becomes a ken, if soft a sighel. The "th" must become thorn, not tyr and hoel. The "ng" sound, as in thing, is the rune ing, not nyd and gyfu.

Second, you don't have to use a Germanic tongue. English is fine.

Third, you will have to contain your incantation in some manner. This can be as simple as drawing (magically as well as physically) a box around your incantation—rather like the borders on the pages of old-fashioned books, including a number of grimoires. Or you may wish to draw on the power of the four dwarves of the cardinal directions. The means of doing this is described in Chapter 8. When using their power to contain an incantation you would simply draw the rune ken at the top, bottom, and the middle of each side of each page of the spell you've written.

But the most important thing to consider when using runes in either monograms or spells is their numeric and color values.

NUMBER AND COLOR

In Chapter 3 I gave numeric and color correspondences for each rune. These are far more than devices for meditative comparison. The numerology of the runes, which is bound with the color correspondences, is worth a book in itself. It is a facet it shares with only one other magical alphabet.

Although each rune has a color, when combined in monograms we do not give each rune its own color, and do so in written text only in one circumstance.

To decide the color of a monogram or spell you first have to decide the general purpose of the rite, and from that determine to which of the aettir it belongs. The attributions of the aettir are given below.

Freyja for matters of happiness, home, love, comfort (including the money to be comfortable), and living generally.

Heimdall for everything pertaining to achievement, power, and success; money where it has social significance (enough money to change your status or make you famous).

Tir for matters of intellect, understanding, spiritual achievement, attaining justice, and authority.

Next, take all the runes in the monogram or inscription and total their numeric value. If you have based a monogram on a phrase, do not count runes from the phrase but from the monogram. Duplicate runes are ignored.

Then turn to the aett of the intent of the magic. The color of the rune of that number is the color you need.

Say you are using Heimdall's aett and the number involved is six. The sixth rune of the aett is poerdh. Since poerdh is red, that is the color you need. In this case it does not matter whether the rune involved is positive or negative, it is only the color which interests us.

If carved and colored in your imagination, the monogram or spell will be in the color you choose. Similarly a monogram on its own can be drawn in its own color. But the spells are best done with the color as background and the runes themselves in the complementary color. In this case the background would be red and the runes green.

The complementary colors are as follows:

red complements green

orange complements blue

yellow complements purple

white complements black

If the number is nine, then use a gray background and the natural colors of all the runes. If you are using a monogram and the number is nine, then the monogram itself can be gray. This can be dark grey on white or light gray on black.

As an example, consider the monogram for inspiration which uses the runes gyfu, boerc, sighel, wynn, and doerg. Numerologically this comes out as follows:

ᚷ ᛒ ᛋ ᚹ ᛗ

$$7 + 2 + 8 + 8 + 8 = 33, 3 + 3 = 6$$

The aett, in this case, is Tir because it is understanding we seek, so the sixth rune is ing and ing is colored black. This monogram should be colored black.

THE AETTIR AGAIN

Back in Chapter 3 we discussed the aettir and their meaning for the Futhark. You may wonder why the aettir have an influence on the use of runes in the monograms or incantations.

For the incantations, simply write down the text; the aettir have no effect. But when dealing with the monograms they can have an importance.

The effect is less with the monograms built from the letters of a statement, if only because the choice of runes is limited. With monograms based on the symbolic value of the runes, however, there are some rules of "aett etiquette" to consider.

When you've set the purpose, choose an aett to decide the color of the monogram. However, that aett also sets the style in which you will provide the sacrifice to maintain the ecological balance the runes require. When I say the rune for writing inspiration is black by looking at the aett of Tir, I also have to accept the kind of price Tir would want for the inspiration provided. In this case, a period of meditation of only a few minutes holds the balance.

For monograms of both symbolic and phrasal origin, keep dark runes apart and at the bottom of the monogram. In symbolic monograms you should avoid using multiple dark runes, but it can be unavoidable in some cases—e.g., ur and nyd over thorn to show that untamed power when harnessed overcomes an enemy.

Be aware that runes of similar function do not always work in the same way. The runes of the later aett are usually wider in scope and affect a greater area of life than their predecessors. One simple check to see if you have chosen the right runes is to use one of your meditative techniques.

Turn all the runes of your monogram into a story to fit the purpose of your spell. If the runes don't fit easily into this context, you may have made the wrong choice.

If you find several runes overlap you may discover that the monogram is working in an ill-defined fashion because it hasn't been given clear instructions. It may seem feoh and odel means great wealth that provides comfort and status, but it doesn't always work that way. You may find money comes but does not provide comfort, or comfort is provided but it isn't you who has the money.

It is better to choose one rune for each area and work the symbolism from that. The task of a monogram is to achieve a result, not model the universe. Choose runes that reinforce your message, not counteract it.

Be careful about combining certain runes. These include eoh and boerc, feoh and odel, nyd and tyr (unless you're willing to take the consequences), tyr and sighel (leads to conflict), or feoh and os.

It is possible to combine these runes if a third rune or other runes form a buffer between them. By themselves tyr and sighel lead to conflict, but when wynn is added to them in a dominant position (either on top or at the center), the monogram instead leads to wisdom of tactics, skill in strategy, and the glory of victory which requires a minimum of actual conflict.

ᛗᛗᛚᛉᛞᚠᚢᛞᚠᚱᚳᚷᛈᚻᛁᛖᛋᚴᚣᛋᛏᛒᛗᛗᛚᛉᛞᚠᚢᛞᚠᚱᚳᚷᛈᚻᛁᛖᛋ

When you combine a few runes, look at their colors. The same colors tend to indicate similar areas of effect. Colors that clash may signal that the runes should not be combined. Colors that work well together are more likely to look good together. Any of the primary colors (red, yellow, blue) in combination, or a primary and a secondary color (green or purple) in combination work well. Complements tend to counteract each other, so red and green runes tend to cancel each other out. Gyfu and ur, gyfu and eoh, and poerdh and lagu all counteract each other, generally weakening the monogram.

White and black runes tend to form a middle ground between runes which, because of color structure, may not go well together. Thus rad makes gyfu and eoh more compatible; isa helps poerdh and lagu work in harness.

FINAL NOTES

With these simple rules you can build monograms and spells to achieve specific tasks for your runic magic. You can use them anywhere, but there are many people who would prefer to perform their rune magic in a special place. It is to the runeplace we turn next.

CHAPTER EIGHT

YOUR RUNEPLACE

Throughout this work we have dealt with magic with a minimum of ceremony. At each stage we have kept magical tools and places out of the subject.

But the Germanic pagans used both tools of magic and sacred places. The use of caves as places of initiation, the building of places of worship, and the existence of sacred groves are all recorded in literature or found at archaeological sites. Tacitus, for example, tells us that the Aclis were worshiped in forest sanctuaries.

In other cases, usually during later eras, there were buildings devoted to religious functions among the pagans. We know that Freyer had churches—the founding of one in Iceland is recorded in some detail.

But there are few of us today who have a forest in which to create a sanctuary, or the land on which to build a temple to the pagan gods. Those with even a room to devote can consider themselves dedicated, affluent, or lucky.

We can still use a number of tools or items not only in runic magic, but also in dedication to the ancient pagan gods. In this chapter we'll have a closer look at this side of things for those who wish to carry their efforts just that one step further.

DIRECTION

Christian churches face east, but pagan churches may face east or north. East is the direction of wisdom; north is the direction of power, especially the power of the dead.

Put in other terms, facing east recognizes the solar cult; facing north recognizes the stellar cult. So the direction in which you choose to orient your temple will have an influence on the devotional rites you practice.

This will not be as important if you simply have your items tucked away neatly and just draw them out when you need them. You need then only face the direction you wish.

But if you are going to consecrate a fixed altar or a room, you are going to have to make a choice. There are no rules for this; if intuition doesn't tell you which direction is best for you then perhaps you should wait before setting up a temple. You can, after all, begin with the items themselves, and let experience be your guide.

CLOTHING

We do know that some rituals were practiced in the nude. Some warriors also fought this way. They, like their magical counterparts, were occasionally painted blue. It is possible that within the blue paint were drugs which led the warriors on a rampage. In later eras they wore identifiable clothes including shirts of bear skin, leading to their name—the bear sarks or berserks.

Tacitus records that priests of the Aclis wore women's apparel. He was quite possibly referring to a loose shift, a shirt which covered the priest to the knees or the ankles. This was one of many types of apparel worn by the pagan priests, and is an easy one to make for yourself.

You simply need a bolt of white cloth. Make certain it isn't a synthetic or synthetic mix: religious garb should always be of natural fibers.

Cut a hole in the cloth for your head and put it on. Have someone mark the hem at a comfortable length. If you have a long bolt don't start in the middle, measure out the front so you will have a proper length.

When you've cut the cloth to the proper length, you'll have to fold the end over to make a hem. Pin it into place and iron it. Then sew it down. It is best if you fold the cloth over twice, so the frayable end of the cloth is entirely sealed away. If you leave a little more than three inches (or eight centimeters) for this you should do fine.

When the hem is finished stitch up the sides of the bolt of cloth, leaving a reasonable space for your arms. This is a very rough-and-ready approach, but it is serviceable, if not very elegant. If you wish to do more, when you cut the hole for your head (before any sewing), don't simply cut a slit, cut a shape like a capital T with the stem going down the front of the shirt.

Fold the cloth in half and trim away from the stem with scissors. It is helpful to use a pencil and a ruler to get an even line. The stem of the T should now be open, somewhat more like a V.

Buy some ribbon (preferably red, but yellow will do). Fold this about in half and iron it to give it a crisp edge. Be certain to buy ribbon which can be ironed. Place one end of the ribbon on one end of the back cut and sew it on. When it's sewn in, trim off the remaining ribbon. Do the same with the other cuts. You should now have a red collar on your white shift.

Before sewing the hem, cut the corners diagonally by about two and a half inches (six centimeters). This will give you the space to make a hem along the bottom and the sides. Again, when sewing, leave a reasonable space for the sleeves, only this time you will make the sleeves.

Get someone to measure the distance from the end of the sleeve hole down to the end of your wrist. Then measure around of your bicep. Add about one and a half to two and a half inches (four to six centimeters) to all these measurements and mark two rectangles of this size on the remaining cloth. If you want the cuffs to fit more tightly, then you'll need to take a measurement of the cuff with the width you want.

ᚠᚢᚦᚨᚱᚲᚷᚹᚺᚾᛁᛃᛇᛈᛉᛊᛏᛒᛖᛗᛚᛜᛞᚠᚢᚦᚨᚱᚲᚷᚹᚺᚾᛁᛃᛊᛏᛒ

If this seems unworkable, get an old long-sleeved shirt and pull apart the sleeves. Either resew them on to your ritual shirt (a bad idea) or use the measurements of the sleeves for your new sleeves.

However, if you're using the basic rectangles, simply hem them as you did the body of the shirt. Roll the rectangle so hem meets hem lengthwise, pin it to hold it in place, and sew this up. You now have the tube of the sleeve. The cuff of this can be given a red ribbon border just as was the collar.

With both sleeve and shirt inside out, sew the sleeve onto the shirt. You'll have to position it and hold it in place with pins. Be prepared to pull a few stitches out to resew them if it feels too tight around the armpit.

With that you have a special garment for your runic magic.

WAND

Most forms of magic have some version of a wand. Germanic paganism is no exception. There are several designs available, from the simple wand carved with runes to the two- or three-pronged wand which eventually evolved into the trident of Paracelsus.

The wood for the wand can be any of a variety of woods: birch, yew, lemonwood, maple, or oak. You can use any kind of pine or fir tree plus the traditional woods. Australian karri, redwood, and eucalyptus (bluegums, especially) are also suitable for magical purposes. But be careful with sheoak; it can be a very powerful wood and is better for pentacles.

If you want a plain wand you can have one made and the proper runes carved in for you. It should be about the same length as the distance from your elbow to the tip of your middle finger and about as thick as the last joint on your middle finger.

Along its side you should carve a flat surface into which you can carve and color or have carved and colored an appropriate inscription of runes. This can be in the form of a monogram, runes chosen for ideographic reasons, or an actual inscription. For example, at the top of the next page is a wand inscribed with

ᚠ · ᛋᚨᚢᛒᛖᚱ · ᚨᚢᛋ · ᚠᚱᛖ� · ᚠ :

"zauber aus Freyer" (magic of Freyer). Note that the inscription begins and ends with the rune feoh. Whenever carving an inscription of words of any length, this rune starts off every line and finishes the last line.

You may wish to use one of the forked wands. These were considered especially useful for healing. In this the length of the wand is the same as before—about as long as the distance from your elbow to the tip of your middle finger. But it should be a bit bigger around, about the diameter of your first two fingers.

Again, you'll need to make a flat surface on which to place the runes. But the choice of runes does not have to be the same as for a straight wand. You may, for example, choose three runes of the same color or numeric value or simply three which are appropriate to your scheme for the use of the wand.

Below is a three-branched wand. On its ends are what the reader may have guessed are my three favorite runes—ken, sighel, and doerg. On the handle of the wand is a runic monogram representing wynn and lagu (from the depths, wisdom).

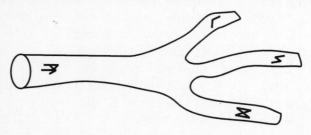

The wand is used for inscribing runes in the air or delineating boundaries. It carries your magical charge, helping to concentrate it in its use.

ᚠᚢᚦᚱᚲᚷᚹᚺᚾᛁ◊ᛃᚲᛦᛋᛏᛒᛖᛗᛚ◊ᛗᚠᚢᚦᚱᚲᚷᚹᚺᚾᛁ◊ᛃᚲᛦᛋᛏᛒ

ARM RING

You may wish to have an arm ring as a symbol of binding oath. If so, it should be made of silver. It can be plain or inscribed with runes to indicate devotion to a god, to the runes, or to your work.

When you put it on, you are symbolically accepting the binding nature of the oath you make in the runes inscribed on the ring. If there are no runes, the plain silver ring is carved with an oath through consecration.

When the oath is fulfilled (if it is a temporary one like a particular series of projections), the ring must be deconsecrated and later consecrated to a new oath.

BINDING THONG

Another device for binding or oaths is the binding thong. Some very simple but effective magic can be made with the help of this simple device.

The thong is a piece of leather or rope with a loop at one end. Through this loop you pass the other end of the thong like a thread through a needle. Tie the loose end in a sturdy, thick knot so it can't slip back through the loop. The length is up to you. Traditionally it was wide enough to slip over yourself so it could wrap around the waist. In this form it is still used in India and Iran among the Brahmans and Zoroastrians. It can be worn as a symbol of dedication and eternity. In a smaller form it can take the place of the silver arm ring.

If it is not worn, you can tie a slip knot in it while reciting a prayer or spell. The knot is then left for nine days. On each of those days the magic should be replenished with prayers or appropriate runes. When the nine days have passed, the slip knot is pulled free and the wish will come true. This should only be used for minor magic or small wishes.

Another form of magic is to place a symbolic object in the thong and pull the loop shut. Hold the end with the knot and magically control what the object represents.

The item in the loop can be money (to attract money), a doll (controlling a person—but only for things like healing or you can get into magical trouble), or other items.

NECKLACE

A necklace of amber beads is useful not only as an item of sacred apparel (particularly in devotion to Freyja), but also to provide a method for keeping track of chanting.

Each time you say a chant or affirmation, move your fingers along one bead. When you've reached the end of the string you know how many chants you've done.

If you want to chant a certain number of times, count back from the clasp as many beads as you wish to do chants. Move your fingers forward for each chant; when you reach the clasp, you're done.

ALTAR

The altar was less central to Germanic pagan traditions than to those of the Middle East. But it was still necessary to have something on which to rest offerings, before which to take oaths, and so on.

For an altar all you really need is a table of wood or wood and metal. No plastics or laminated coverings should be used. However, a folding table will do, and in such case the clips holding it in position can be made of plastic.

You can drape a cloth over it. If this is done, it should be white and unadorned with any pattern or borders.

The main question is simply whether you will face it north or east. If you're in the southern hemisphere you may wish to substitute south for north, since in this hemisphere the directional star is over the south pole.

PILLAR

You may wish to have a pillar in your temple, particularly if you have a room set aside for your magic. This is not representative of the twin pillars Boaz and Jachin, which derive ultimately from the twin pillars of Solomon's temple, but it is a single pillar bearing architectural wings representing the world pillar, or Yggdrasil, the World Tree. This idea of the world being held up by a pillar or tree is very ancient: as we've seen, it may predate modern humanity.

The method of constructing this pillar can vary widely. The pillar can be a treated pine pole such as is used for building some fences. It can be a circular lintel, or you can make it out of cardboard and papier-mâché.

Wrap a piece of flexible cardboard into a tube and tape it into place. If you want your construction to be sturdy, add more layers to the roll. The pillar can be anything from a single layer to a solid post.

When you have your first length, wrap another layer. Link these two by taping them together. Keep doing this until you have a pillar of the height you want. Remember, though, it will have to be taller than you.

When you've got the length, trim some more cardboard so you have strips no longer than your hand from base to middle finger tip. Wrap these around one end of the pillar and tape them in place. This will form the base of the pillar; you will need several layers to keep the structure stable.

At the top of the structure you will need to put wings to indicate that it is a supportive structure. These can be wooden beams cut at an angle at one end and nailed together. Then a groove or joint is cut in the pillar at the top. This joint has to be the width of the wooden beams plus a millimeter.

The wood then fits into the slot. The angle of the wood depends on the angle of the cut you make. It should be between 30 and 45 degrees.

If you prefer, roll up some more of the cardboard tightly. Tape it in a roll and cut the end as you would with the beams. Tape the two ends together and join them to the pillar as before.

Once you have this structure completed, cut newspaper into strips. Then get a large bowl of paste. Dip the newspaper into the paste and apply this to the pillar.

When you've covered the whole pillar, let it dry. Repeat the process until you have the pillar covered with about three to four layers of papier-mâché. Then paint the pillar brown, the base black, and the beams at the top a light brown or yellow.

You can also put a device on the front of the pillar. A nail will remind you of Thor (iron hit with flint will cause sparks, a reference to lightning). The rune tyr will refer to Tiwaz. A ship is Njord. And so on. The decoration of the pillar will be largely up to you.

CAULDRON AND DRINKING HORN

Either or both of these devices can be used in your magical pursuits. They are both suitable for skrying and ritual use. The cauldron refers to plenty, the oath of community, and wisdom. The drinking horn is a similar device on a more personal scale. But the cauldron is the generative power of woman while the horn is brotherhood, so the two are different in their approach to seemingly similar blessings.

Both will hold beer for drinking, or water for ritually cleansing or (with ink added) skrying.

The end of the drinking horn must come to a tip and not have a base like a normal drinking glass. It must also have two legs so, with the tip, it can stand on its own. Alternatively it can have a separate stand on which it can rest. It should hold about two cups of liquid.

The cauldron should be as round as possible and have an identifiable neck and three legs rather like a Celtic cromlech, if possible. Any inscription on the cauldron should be placed on its neck. It will, of course, have to be dedicated to a female god.

YOUR RUNEPLACE

The Germanic pagans had far more opportunity than most of us have to have carts, processions, and other things we associate with paganism. If you have a space in a room or a room itself to devote to runic magic you may be wondering how best to decorate it.

Largely this is a matter of choice, though there are some general rules.

If you have a pillar, it must be placed in the north. It represents the pillar that holds up the sky, and hence must be aligned with the north star. It is magically acceptable to put it in the middle of the room, but this tends to leave little space for other activities.

Don't put the pillar right in front of a window. This tends to give the pillar a blackish appearance against the light. If you have curtains or blinds which are truly effective or if you will only use your runeplace at night then this is no problem.

The pillar doesn't have to be exactly at true north (either magnetic or geographic). But beyond northeast or northwest is too far. Fortunately it does not matter whether the pillar is at a wall or a corner, but if possible set it in the center of a wall or the center of a corner.

Next comes the placement of the altar. This should face the pillar in the north, so that you face the pillar when you stand at the altar. If the altar faces east, then when you stand at it the pillar will be on your left, which is not acceptable.

When not in use the items of magic such as horn, cauldron, and so on should be on or under the altar, or wrapped in a white cloth of linen or cotton (do not use synthetic fabrics).

CONSECRATION RITE

The only thing remaining is the consecration of your runeplace and its equipment. In this you should know that there were four guardians, dwarves who held the edges of the skull which was the sky. These were Nordi in the North, Austri in the East, Vesti in the West, and Sudri in the South.

For each direction carve and color the rune ken before reciting the following:

> *[Dwarf] of the [direction],*
> *see thee the light of the torch,*

ᛗᛗᚲᛜᚹᚾᛏᚦᚱᚲᛉᛈᚺᛡᛂ ᛋᚲᚤᛏᛒᛗᛗᚲᛜᚹᚾᛏᚦᚱᚲᛉᛈᚺᛡᛂᛋ

accept its flame
and let none pass thee by,
lest it scorch them to death.

Start with the north and move clockwise. If and only if your altar faces east may you start with that direction.

If you wish to visualize the dwarves in question, this can be done. They all look alike with studded metal helmets and animal-skin or leather jerkins, breeches, and boots.

Nordi is dark, Austri is yellow, Sudri is red, and Vestri is green or blue. This is not a solid coloring, but a tint.

Then over each item you will use draw lagu, then splash some water on it. The water can just be a few drops applied with your fingers. With each splash, say:

With this water
I ready thee
for the magic
for which thou will be used.

Then dry the item and wrap it in its cloth.

To sanctify your runeplace as a whole, set the four dwarves to guard again (do this every time you start work in the rune-place) and inscribe in each of the four cardinal directions, plus a special magical monogram toward all doors and windows.

This monogram is based on your name or your magical name if you have one. This will ensure that the runes establish this place as yours, with your magic, and your destiny setting forth from this point.

When you are done with your magic dismiss the dwarves. First erase ken, then say:

[Dwarf] of [direction],
I thank thee for thy work.
Blessings to thee
and farewell
until we meet again.

ᚠᚢᚦᚨᚱᚲᚷᚹᚻᚾᛁᛃᛇᛈᛉᛋᛏᛒᛖᛗᛚᛜᛞᚠᚢᚦᚨᚱᚲᚷᚹᚻᛁᛃᛇᛋᛏᛒ

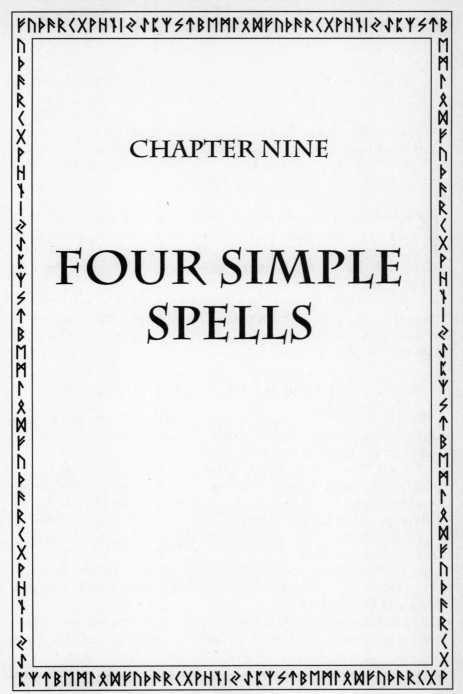

CHAPTER NINE

FOUR SIMPLE
SPELLS

ᚠWhat sort of magic can you perform in your runeplace? Basically, the same sort you can do after reading no more than
Chapter 1. In this chapter we'll look at four simple spells.
These will serve you whether you've only just read Chapter 1 or
if you have a full runeplace.

Each of the spells is flexible in use and method and can
form the core of complex rituals. The purpose here, however, is
to provide you with the basic functional spells which will help
you tap the power of the runes.

THE RUNE ITSELF

When you carve and color a rune, whether in wood or your
imagination, you call up its power. It is only necessary to imagine the rune properly to build psychic momentum.

Start by deciding what you want: money, love, wisdom,
power, whatever. Choose the aett which most closely corre-
sponds to that want. Love and comfort, home and happiness to
Freyja; power to Heimdall; knowledge and things spiritual to Tir.

From within that aett choose the rune that is most appropriate to your wishes.

Then sit down and write out your wish on a piece of paper.
Boil it down to a few simple words, and address it to the god
associated with the rune.

Let's say you find life has too great an effect on you. When
things go wrong you find it difficult to cope. You need a little

more fortitude and a little more courage in your daily life so you won't be so buffeted. This is Freyja's aett; what you want is the test and challenge of thorn.

This rune will lead you toward the cause of your fear. So you need to address your wish as follows:

> *Hel and Nidhogg,*
> *terrible beings,*
> *I turn against your fear.*
> *I call up thorn*
> *that I may see his face*
> *and not fear him again.*

With that you're ready for the spell. You normally have to think of a proper balance, a sacrifice, but in this case the change you seek is already balanced because you will strengthen Freyja's precepts. So you're ready for the spell.

You can carve and color the rune in your imagination or on a piece of paper. If the latter, have something (marker, colored pencil, etc.) with which to draw the rune in its proper color. For carving strokes, hold the writing utensil above the page.

Carve the strokes in the appropriate order. If you haven't memorized them, have the order set out on a separate sheet of paper. Say the appropriate words with each stroke. In this case, "Alone am I when I face danger, but never do I falter."

Next, color the rune. If you have dark-colored paper color it white, otherwise it can be gray on a white background. Again, use the appropriate words for each of the strokes which themselves must be done in the right order.

When you have the rune completed, stand facing the north while holding the rune in front of you. Recite the wish you've made, and then imagine it coming true. When you're done, thank the deity in charge of the aett of the rune you've used. In this case, Freyja:

> *I thank thee, Freyja,*
> *for having heard my prayers,*
> *and know that thou wilt answer them.*

ᛗᛗᛚᛉᛗᚠᚾ�þᚨᚱᚲᚷᛈᚺᛉᛁᚹᛃᛊᚲᛣᛋᛏᛒᛗᛗᛚᛉᛗᚠᚾ�þᚨᚱᚲᚷᛈᚺᛉᛁᚹᛃ

I thank thee for this gift of
[state your wish as having come true].

The "thee" is not an affectation: the term "you" is too vague for addressing a deity.

CANDLE MAGIC

You can use candles for runic magic. There are several means for doing this. First, purchase a candle. It doesn't have to be a taper candle—the pyramid or cone shapes work well. But don't buy a novelty item.

You should, as in the last spell, have already decided which rune you wish to use, and exactly what your wish is.

Get a modeling knife. Into the side of the candle near the base carve the rune you wish to use. Carve the strokes in the right order and with the right words. To color it you can either use wax of the appropriate color or a felt-tip marker. Again, the appropriate words should be spoken.

When this is done you should bless the candle, addressing yourself to the deity of the rune you are using. If you want to use wynn to gain wisdom, you might say:

Skirnir, shining one, messenger of gods,
bless this candle with me
that by its light I shall gain
wisdom.

Here again, the candle is a sacrifice. But if you want wynn to provide preferment or great wisdom, you might add:

To this,
a gift demands a gift,
so I pledge for this wisdom
nine golden [or silver] coins
to the poor.

Australia has gold-colored coins, but nine silver dollars or half-dollars will work as well. The metal in the coins is itself important, so don't use paper money or a credit card.

ᚠᚢᚦᚨᚱᚲᚷᚹᚺᚾᛁᛄᛇᛈᛉᛋᛏᛒᛖᛗᛚᛜᛞᚠᚢᚦᚨᚱᚲᚷᚹᚺᚾᛁᛄᛇᛈᛋᛏᛒ

Then face the north again and light the candle. When it's lit, blow it out. Do this until it has been lit nine times. On the ninth time, leave it lit and let it burn itself out.

If the candle proves faulty—if it snuffs itself, blows out due to a breeze, or burns a channel straight through leaving most of the wax untouched—do the ritual again. You may need to rethink your gift.

BINDING MAGIC

In Chapter 8 I talked of a binding thong. You can use that magic quite easily. Draw the rune on a piece of paper as described in the first spell of this chapter. Roll up the paper and tie a binding thong of twine around it.

Carve and color the rune in the air over the paper, using the strokes in their proper order and the proper words with each stroke.

Now imagine your wish coming true.

Bury the paper. The magic will be slowly released as the paper rots.

This spell can be used for healing someone slowly or sustaining health when the sickness he or she has is too powerful to be cured. It can also bind a malevolent force for a time.

Again, it can be used against the demon thorn. Once bound for a time, you use the opportunity to prepare for the demon's return when you can defeat it. It also slows down human enemies.

It can also be used as a form of oathgiving. Instead of one rune you write out the whole of your oath/wish in runes, bind it, and bury it. The oath will guide your life until the paper and twine rot.

For example, carve and color doerg. Bind the piece of paper and say:

> With this, O Balder, I am bound
> to the light and to the good.
> Guide me in the time this oath allows,
> that I might know the way of light.

When you bury the paper, thank Tir:

I thank thee, Tir,
for thy wisdom and light
which shall come of this oath.

A PIECE OF WOOD

Get a large flat piece of wood and some markers or paint. At the top of the wood carve and color the rune of your wish. Then write the text of your wish on the rest of the board, carving and coloring the whole way.

If the board cannot be physically carved, do the stroke above the wood and color the wood itself.

In this you should have your wish letter-perfect, because the color of the written text must be done in accord with the method given in Chapter 7 on monograms.

You will need to paint the lower part of the wood the color of the combined runes (except the one at the top), and then color the runes themselves the complementary color.

Don't forget that feoh must precede all lines, and end the first and last line. These runes are not used in calculating color. Put a dot between feoh and the line proper and between all words.

When you're done you should have something like the illustration below:

When you're done coloring and carving, address your request to the god associated with the rune. When that's done, imagine that your wish is coming true.

Leave the board for nine days. It can be left on your altar, put in a dark place, or wrapped in a cloth of natural fibers.

Then take out the board and again imagine your wish coming true. Thank the god of the aett of the rune at the top of the board. Then burn the board.

If you want more power, address the god of the rune again, imagine success, wait nine more days, and then burn the board. The more you put off burning, the more power you can raise up to the maximum magical charge you can yourself sustain.

With that you should be ready to practice runic magic.

THE ELDER FUTHARK

Feoh	ᚠ
Ur	ᚢ
Thorn	ᚦ
Os	ᚨ
Rad	ᚱ
Ken	ᚲ
Gyfu	ᚷ
Wynn	ᚹ
Hoel	ᚺ
Nyd	ᚾ
Isa	ᛁ
Ger	ᛃ
Eoh	ᛇ
Poerdh	ᛈ
Eohl	ᛉ
Sighel	ᛋ
Tyr	ᛏ
Boerc	ᛒ
Ehwis	ᛖ
Manu	ᛗ
Lagu	ᛚ
Ing	ᛜ
Odel	ᛟ
Doerg	ᛞ

FURTHER READING

There are a great many books on the runes and an even wider variety on the Germanic myths, a topic we've had little chance to discuss in this work.

The list below provides a selection of some of the better works available at the moment, covering the various topics of this work and more.

ANCIENT REFERENCES

Snorri Sturluson. *The Prose Edda.*

> The source of much of our knowledge of the Germanic myths. Sturlson was a twelfth-century Christian writer who had sympathy with the material of the myths, though it is unlikely that they were anything more than fables to him.

Cornelius Tacitus. *Germania.*

> Though it needs to be treated with caution, this is the longest of accounts on Germanic tribes, their customs, and their religious practices.

Saxo Grammaticus. *Gesta Danorum.*

> A lesser work than the other two, perhaps because of the author's own religious intolerance.

The Elder Edda or *The Poetic Edda.*

> Myths and poems; contains many kennings or allusions, not all of which are clear to us.

All the above are in various translations, any of which the reader will find suitable.

RUNES

Cooper, D. Jason. *Using the Runes.* London: Aquarian Press, 1986.

A companion volume to this, it's designed to be an introduction to the general field of the runes and Germanic paganism.

Howard, Michael. *The Magic of the Runes: Their Origins and Occult Power.* York Beach, ME: Samuel Weiser, 1980.

Howard, Michael. *The Runes and Other Magical Alphabets.* London: Aquarian Press, 1978.

Good works. The first is practical but the latter shows better scholarship.

Thorsson, Edred. *Futhark: A Handbook of Magic.* York Beach, ME: Samuel Weiser, 1984.

Thorsson, Edred. *Northern Magic.* St. Paul, MN: Llewellyn Publications, 1992.

The author is clearly a practicing magician. His works are worthy of note. The first has a small glossary of Norse magical terms.

MYTHOLOGY

Auden, W. H. and Paul B. Taylor. *Norse Poems.* London: The Althlone Press, 1981.

Handy reference. For those who believe in using Norse words, it has a Norse-to-English dictionary.

Branston, Brian. *The Lost Gods of England.* London: Thames and Hudson, 1974.

Most notable for its analysis of the pantheon before the rise of the cult of Odin, this book takes a remarkable look at the Saxon version of the acient myths.

Crossley-Holland, Kevin. *The Norse Myths.* Middlesex, UK: Penguin Books, 1980.

Good reconstruction of the myths told as narrative in (as best as can be done) chronological order. Glossary of Germanic names, places, gods, etc. Good notes, good bibliography.

Dumezil, Geroges. *Gods of the Ancient Northmen*. Berkeley, CA: University of California Press, 1946.

Collected essays, edited by Einar Haugen, introduction by Scott Littleton and Udo Strutynski. It is a pity most of Dumezil's work is still in French awaiting translation.

Ellis-Davidson, H. R. *Gods and Myths of Northern Europe*. Middlesex: Penguin Books, 1964.

Ellis-Davidson, H. R. *Pagan Scandinavia*. London: Thames and Hudson, 1967.

The first book is a standard introduction to the Germanic myths. It is clearly reasoned and keeps as much as possible to proven ground. Professor Ellis-Davidson has a pronounced sympathy with the myths of ancient peoples. The second work gives a look at a different branch of Germanic mythology. It shows, among other things, how ancient and widespread the worship of Tiwaz was. This work concentrates on Bronze Age beliefs.

Martin, Stanley John. *Ragnarok: An Investigation into the Old Norse Concepts of the Fate of the Gods*. Assen, Netherlands: Van Gorcum & Co., 1972.

Shows that the myths handed down to us were not the myths of the height of Germanic paganism.

Ward, Donald. *The Divine Twins: An Indo-European Myth in Germanic Tradition*. Berkeley and Los Angeles, CA: University of California Press, 1968.

To be read especially for details of the Aclis with the implications for the rune Ehwis.

ASTRAL PROJECTION

Brennan, J. H. *Astral Projection*. London: Aquarian Press, 1971.

Brennan, J. H. *Discover Astral Projection*. London: Aquarian Press, 1989.

The former is an excellent introduction to projection through the symbols, while the latter is a wider study.

ᛗᛖᛚᛉᛗᚠᚢᛈᚦᚨᚱᚲᚷᛈᚺᚾᛁᛞᛊᛚᚲᛃᛋᛏᛒᛗᛗᛚᛉᛗᚠᚢᛈᚦᚨᚱᚲᚷᛈᚺᚾᛁᛞᛊ

Denning, Melita and Osborne Phillips. *Magical States of Consciousness*. St. Paul, MN: Llewellyn Publications, 1985.

A description of a branch of astral projection called pathworking. This work confines itself to the (spiritually) easier of the paths.

COLOR SYMBOLISM

Ousley, S. G. J. *Colour Meditations*. Romford, Essex, UK: L. N. Fowler and Co., 1951.

Ousley, S. G. J. *The Power of the Rays: The Science of Color-Healing*. Romford, Essex, UK: L. N. Fowler and Co., 1951.

Two basic introductions, one leaning to theory, the other to practice.

NUMBER SYMBOLISM

Cooper, D. Jason. *Understanding Numerology*. London: Aquarian Press, 1986.

An introductory work, but it does provide new concepts.

Iamblichus. *The Theology of Arithmetic: On the Mystical, Mathematical and Cosmological Symbolism of the First Ten Numbers*. Robin Waterfield, trans. Grand Rapids, MI: Phanes Press, 1988.

Iamblichus was a writer during the time of the Roman Empire. He was a Pythagorean philosopher whose work has influenced numerology—directly or indirectly—for centuries.

Westcott, W. Wynn. *Numbers: Their Occult Power and Mystic Virtues*. London: Theosophical Society Publishing House, 1890.

A perennial classic, simple to understand because it emphasizes example rather than theory and provides a good grounding. Reprinted every few years.

INDEX

ᚠᚢᚦᚨᚱᚲᚷᚹᚺᚾᛁᛃᛇᛈᛉᛊᛏᛒᛗᛘᛚᛜᛞᚠᚢᚦᚨᚱᚲᚷᚹᚺᚾᛁᛃᛇᛈᛉᛊᛏᛒ

ᛗᛗᚠᛉᛗᚹᚠᛝᚦᚱᛈᚷᛈᚺᛁᛈᛇᛁᚲᛃᛥᛒᛗᛗᚠᛉᛗᚹᚠᛝᚦᚱᛈᚷᛈᚺᛁᛈᛇ

ᚠᚢᚦᚫᚱᚲᚷᚹᚺᚾᛁᛂᛃᛈᛇᛏᛒᛖᛗᛚᛜᚠᚢᚦᚫᚱᚲᚷᚹᚺᚾᛁᛂᛃᛈᛇᛏᛒ

STAY IN TOUCH

To obtain our full catalog, to keep informed about new titles as they are released and to benefit from informative articles and helpful news, you are invited to write for our bimonthly news magazine/catalog, *Llewellyn's New Worlds of Mind and Spirit*. A sample copy is free, and it will continue coming to you at no cost as long as you are an active mail customer. Or you may subscribe for just $10.00 in U.S.A. and Canada ($20.00 overseas, first class mail). Many bookstores also have New Worlds available to their customers. Ask for it.

Stay in touch! In *New Worlds'* pages you will find news and features about new books, tapes and services, announcements of meetings and seminars, articles helpful to our readers, news of authors, products and services, special money-making opportunities, and much more.

Llewellyn's New Worlds of Mind and Spirit
P.O. Box 64383-K174, St. Paul, MN 55164-0383, U.S.A.

* * *

TO ORDER BOOKS AND TAPES

You may order books directly from the publisher by sending full price in U.S. funds, plus $3.00 for postage and handling for orders under $10.00; $4.00 for orders over $10.00. There are no postage and handling charges for orders over $50.00. Postage and handling rates are subject to change. UPS Delivery: We ship UPS whenever possible. Delivery guaranteed. Provide your street address as UPS does not deliver to P.O. Boxes. UPS to Canada requires a $50.00 minimum order. Allow 4-6 weeks for delivery. Orders outside the U.S.A. and Canada: Airmail—add retail price of book; add $5.00 for each non-book item (tapes, etc.); add $1.00 per item for surface mail.

FOR GROUP STUDY AND PURCHASE

Because there is a great deal of interest in group discussion and study of the subject matter of this book, we feel that we should encourage the adoption and use of this particular book by such groups by offering a special quantity price to group leaders or agents.

Our special quantity price for a minimum order of five copies of *Esoteric Rune Magic* is $36.00 cash-with-order. This price includes postage and handling within the United States. Minnesota residents must add 6.5% sales tax. For additional quantities, please order in multiples of five. For Canadian and foreign orders, add postage and handling charges as above. Credit card (VISA, MasterCard, American Express) orders are accepted. Charge card orders only ($15.00 minimum order) may be phoned in free within the U.S.A. or Canada by dialing 1-800-THE-MOON. For customer service, call 1-612-291-1970. Mail orders to:

LLEWELLYN PUBLICATIONS
P.O. Box 64383-K174, St. Paul, MN 55164-0383, U.S.A.

All prices subject to change without notice.

THE POWER OF THE RUNES
A Complete Kit for Divination & Magic
by Donald Tyson

This kit contains *Rune Magic,* Tyson's highly acclaimed guide to effective runework. In this book he clears away misconceptions surrounding this magical alphabet of the Northern Europeans, provides information on the Gods and Goddesses of the runes, and gives the meanings and uses of all 33 extant runes. The reader will be involved with practical runic rituals and will find advice on talisman, amulet and sigil use.

This kit also includes the Rune Magic Deck. This set of 24 large cards illustrates each of the Futhark runes in a stunning 2-color format. This is the first deck ever published, which makes it not only unique, but truly historical! In addition, there is a set of four wooden rune dice in their own cloth bag. These square dice were designed by Donald Tyson himself. The user casts them down, then interprets their meanings as they appear before him. With the 24 Futhark runes graphically etched on their sides, these dice let the user perform an accurate reading in mere seconds.

0-87542-828-2, Boxed set: *Rune Magic,*
24-card deck, 4 dice w/bag $24.95

THE NINE DOORS OF MIDGARD
A Complete Curriculum of Rune Magic
by Edred Thorsson

The Nine Doors of Midgard are the gateways to self-transformation through the runes. This is the complete course of study and practice which has successfully been in use inside the Rune-Gild for ten years. Now it is being made available to the public for the first time.

The runic tradition represents a whole school of magic with the potential of becoming the equal of the Hermetic or Cabalistic tradition. The runic tradition is the northern or Teutonic equivalent of the Hermetic tradition of the south. *The Nine Doors of Midgard* is the only manual to take a systematic approach to initiation into runic practices.

Through nine lessons or stages in a graded curriculum, the books takes the rune student from a stage in which no previous knowledge of runes or esoteric work is assumed to a fairly advanced stage of initiation. The book also contains a complete reading course in outside material.

0-87542-781-2, 320 pgs., 5¼ x 8, illus. $12.95

All prices subject to change without notice.

LEAVES OF YGGDRASIL
Runes, Gods, Magic, Feminine Mysteries, Folklore
by Freya Aswynn

Leaves of Yggdrasil is the first book to offer an extensive presentation of Rune concepts, mythology and magical applications inspired by Dutch/Frisian traditional lore.

Author Freya Aswynn, although writing from a historical perspective, offers her own interpretations of this data based on her personal experience with the system. Freya's inborn, native gift of psychism enables her to work as a runic seer and consultant in psychological rune readings, one of which is detailed in a chapter on "Runic Divination."

Leaves of Yggdrasil emphasizes the feminine mysteries and the function of the Northern priestesses. It unveils a complete and personal system of the rune magic that will fascinate students of mythology, spirituality, psychism and Teutonic history, for this is not only a religious autobiography but also a historical account of the ancient Northern European culture.

0-87542-024-9, 288 pgs., 5¼ x 8, softcover $12.95

NORSE MAGIC
by D. J. Conway

The Norse: adventurous Viking wanderers, daring warriors, worshipers of the Aesir and the Vanir. Like the Celtic tribes, the Northmen had strong ties with the Earth and Elements, the Gods and "little people."

Norse Magic is an active magic, only for participants, not bystanders. It is a magic of pride in oneself and the courage to face whatever comes. It interests those who believe in shaping their own future, those who believe that practicing spellwork is preferable to sitting around passively waiting for changes to come.

The book leads the beginner step by step through the spells. The in-depth discussion of Norse deities and the Norse way of life and worship set the intermediate student on the path to developing his or her own active rituals. *Norse Magic* is a compelling and easy-to-read introduction to the Norse religion and Teutonic mythology. The magical techniques are refreshingly direct and simple, with a strong feminine and goddess orientation.

0-87542-137-7, 240 pgs., mass market, illus. $3.95

All prices subject to change without notice.

NORTHERN MAGIC
Mysteries of the Norse, Germans & English
by Edred Thorsson

This in-depth primer of the magic of the Northern Way introduces the concepts and practices of Gothic or Germanic magic. English, German, Dutch, Icelandic, Danish, Norwegian, and Swedish peoples are all directly descended from this ancient Germanic cultural stock. According to author Edred Thorsson, if you are interested in living a holistic life with unity of body-mind-spirit, a key to knowing your spiritual heritage is found in the heritage of your body—in the natural features which you have inherited from your distant ancestors. Most readers of this book already "speak the language" of the Teutonic tradition.

Northern Magic contains material that has never before been discussed in a practical way. This book outlines the ways of Northern magic and the character of the Northern magician. It explores the theories of traditional Northern psychology (or the lore of the soul) in some depth, as well as the religious tradition of the Troth and the whole Germanic theology. The remaining chapters make up a series of "mini-grimoires" on four basic magical techniques in the Northern Way: Younger Futhark rune magic, Icelandic galdor staves, Pennsylvania hex signs, and "seith" (or shamanism). This is an excellent overview of the Teutonic tradition that will interest neophytes as well as long-time travelers along the Northern Way.

0-87542-782-0, 224 pgs., mass market, illus.   **$4.95**

PRACTICAL COLOR MAGICK
by Raymond Buckland, Ph.D.

Color magick is powerful—and safe. Here is a sourcebook for the psychic influence of color on our physical lives. Contains complete rituals and meditations for practical applications of color magick for health, success and love. Find full instructions on how to meditate more effectively and use color to stimulate the chakras and unfold psychic abilities. Learn to use color in divination and in the making of talismans, sigils and magick squares.

This book will teach all the powers of light and more. You'll learn new forms of expression of your innermost self, new ways of relating to others with the secret languages of light and color. Put true color back into your life with the rich spectrum of ideas and practical magical formulas from *Practical Color Magick!*

0-87542-047-8, 160 pgs., illus., softcover   **$6.95**

All prices subject to change without notice.